50 Easy Classical Guitar pieces

Compiled and edited by
Dmitrijs Volkovs

Access to Online Audio
https://esmistudio.com/guitarbook1.zip

Copyright © 2024 Dmitrijs Volkovs

ISBN: **978-1-7637136-0-4**

CONTENTS

1 Renaissance Era Composers

3 What if a day, or a month, or a year *(Anonymous)*
4 Branle anglaise *(Emmanuel Adriansen)*
5 Canary dance *(Anonymous)*
6 Greensleeves *(Anonymous)*
7 Pavane *(Anonymous)*
9 Allemande *(Anonymous)*
10 Pezzo Tedesco *(Anonymous)*
11 Toy *(Francis Cutting)*
12 Packington's Pound *(Francis Cutting)*
14 Mr. Dowland's Midnight *(John Dowland)*
15 Orlando Sleepeth *(John Dowland)*

15 Baroque Era Composers

20 Aria *(Henry Purcell)*
21 Paradetas *(Gaspar Sanz)*
22 Rujero *(Gaspar Sanz)*
23 Bourree *(Johann Krieger)*
24 Gigue *(Johann Anton Logy)*
25 Bourree *(Leopold Mozart)*
26 Menuet *(Johann Christoph Friederich Bach)*
27 Menuet *(Johann Krieger)*
29 Menuet *(Robert de Visée)*
30 Menuet *(Silvius Leopold Weiss)*
31 Españoleta *(Gaspar Sanz)*
34 Menuet in G *(Johann Sebastian Bach)*
36 Gigue *(Giuseppe Antonio Brescianello)*
40 Bourrée - *Suite in D minor (Robert de Visée)*

41 Classical Era Composers

44 Andante 1 *(Ferdinando Carulli)*
46 Andante in C *(Fernando Sor)*
47 Andante *(Fernando Sor)*
48 Andantino *(Ferdinando Carulli)*
50 Andantino 2 *(Ferdinando Carulli)*
51 Ecossaise *(Mauro Giuliani)*
52 Allegro *(Mauro Giuliani)*
53 Etude A minor *(Dionisio AGUADO)*
54 Menuet in A minor *(Dionisio Aguado)*
55 Walz *(Dionisio Aguado)*
56 Waltz *(Ferdinando Carulli)*
58 Moderato *(Anton Diabelli)*
59 Andante 2 *(Ferdinando Carulli)*
62 Etude No.9 op.35 *(Fernando Sor)*

65 Romantic Era Composers

68 Allegretto *(Matteo Carcassi)*
70 Allegretto 2 *(Matteo Carcassi)*
72 Andantino *(Matteo Carcassi)*
74 Study in A minor *(Napoleon Coste)*
75 Etude *(Francisco Tarrega)*
77 Etude in G *(Johann Kaspar Mertz)*
78 Ländler *(Johann Kaspar Mertz)*
80 Lagrima *(Francisco Tarrega)*
82 Pastoral *(Matteo Carcassi)*
84 Romance *(Johann Kaspar Mertz)*
86 Study in A minor *(Matteo Carcassi)*

Renaissance Composers

Anonymous

The Renaissance (which means "rebirth or "revival") began around 1400 and ended in the early 1600s. The musicians and artists of the Renaissance looked back to classical models, spawning a new era of artistic growth. With the invention of the printing press, music became available to the public as never before.

John Dowland (1563-1626)

John Dowland was an English Renaissance composer, lutenist, and singer. He is best known today for his melancholy songs such as "Come, heavy sleep", "Come again", "Flow my tears", "I saw my Lady weepe" and "In darkness let me dwell", but his instrumental music has undergone a major revival, and with the 20th century's early music revival, has been a continuing source of repertoire for lutenists and classical guitarists.

Francis Cutting (c.1550–1595/6)

Francis Cutting was an English Lutenist and Composer during the Renaissance period. Renaissance music is European music written during the Renaissance. Defining the beginning of the musical era is difficult, given the gradually adopted "Renaissance" characteristics: musicologists have placed its beginnings from as early as 1300 to as late as the 1470s.

What if a day, or a month, or a year.

Traditional (XVI century)

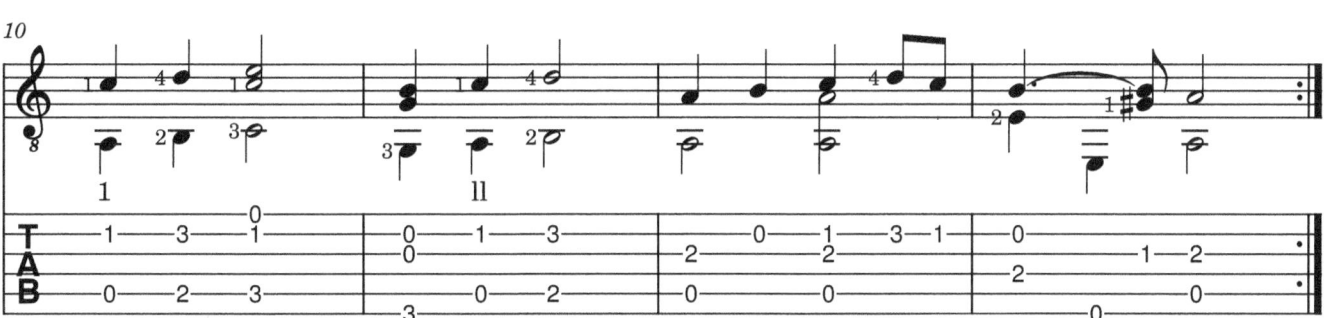

Branle anglais

Emmanuel Adriansen (1550-1604)

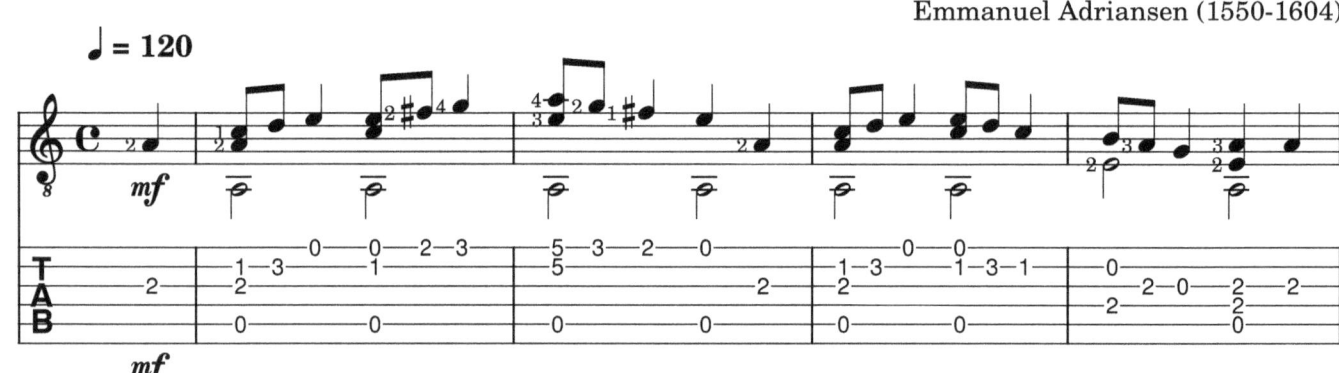

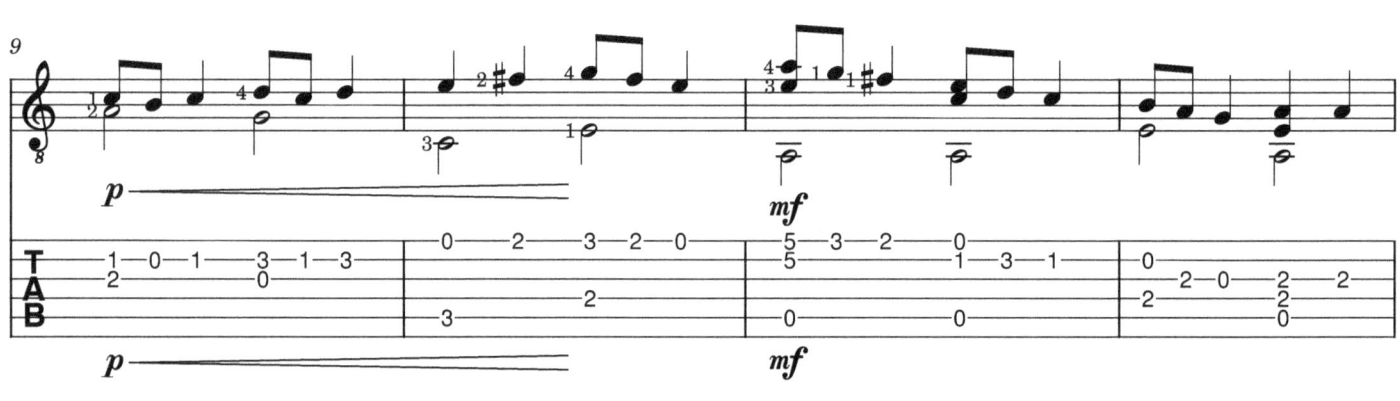
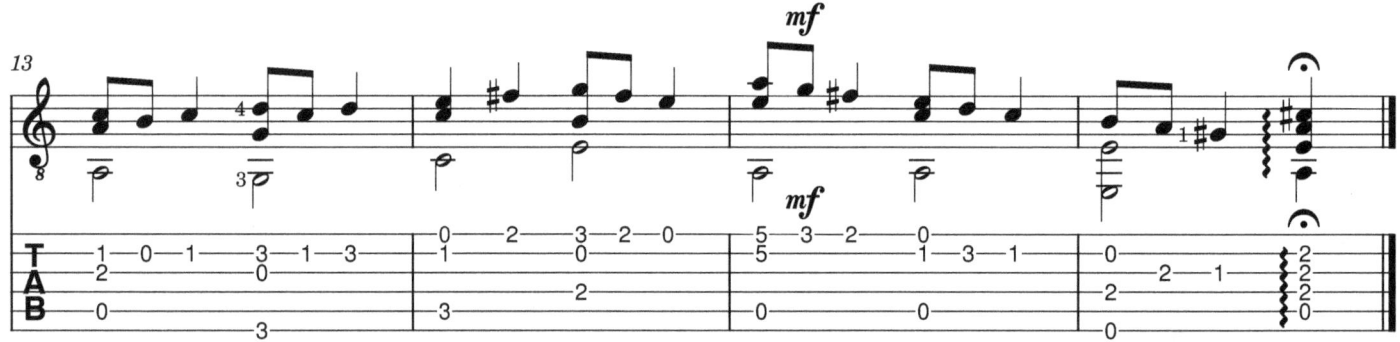

Canary dance

Anonymous (XVIII century)

Greensleeves

16th century English Traditional

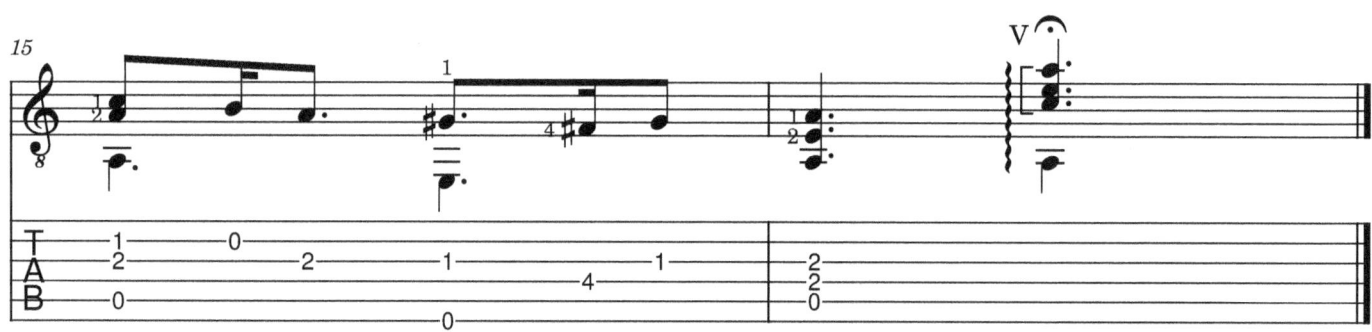

Pavane

Anonymous (XVI century)

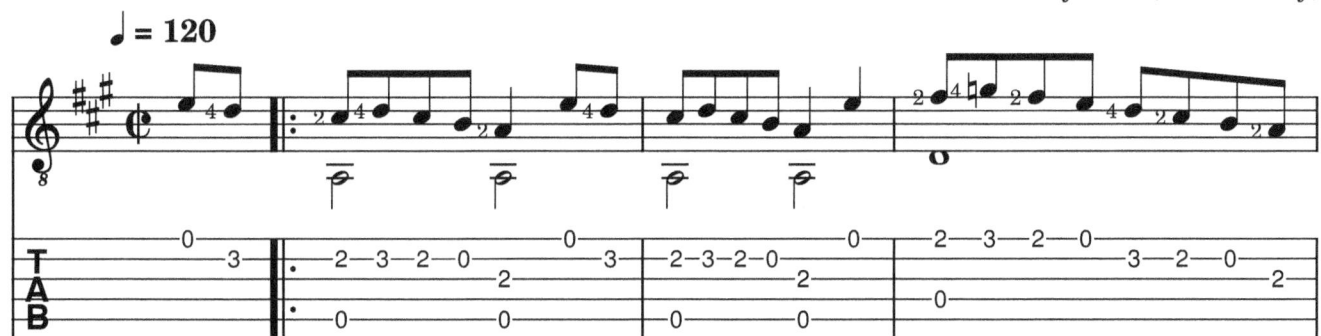
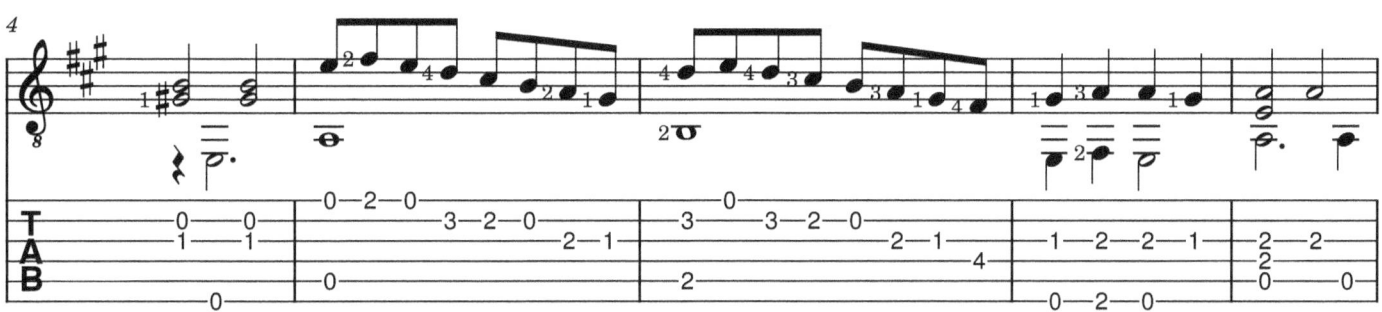
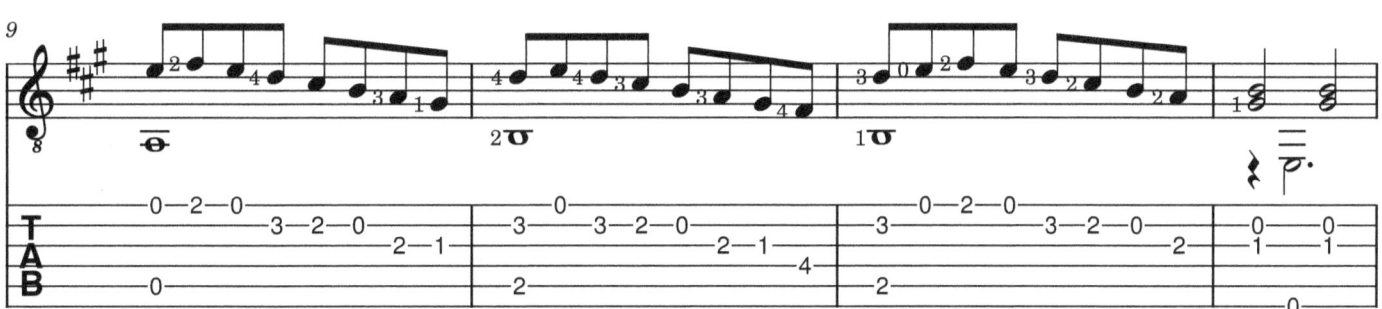
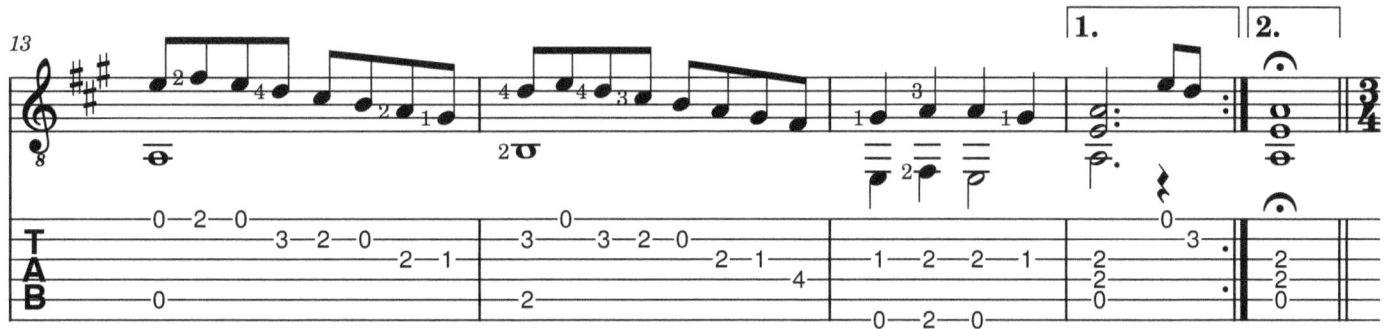

Allemande

Anonymous XVI century

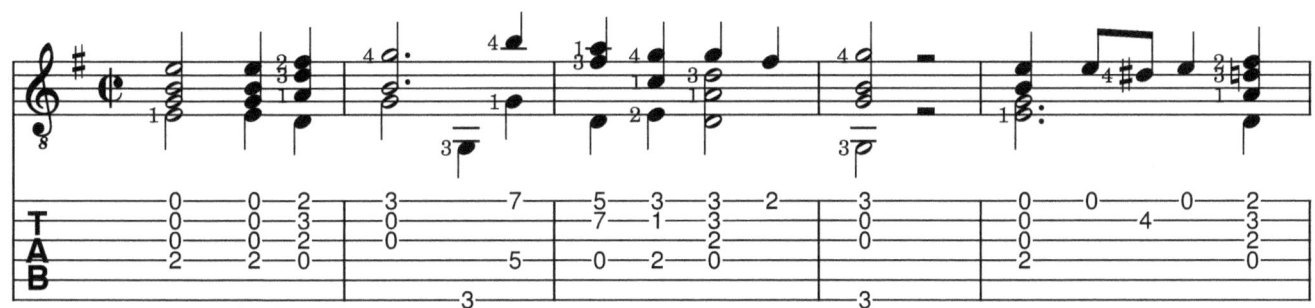

Pezzo Tedesco

Anonymous 16th century

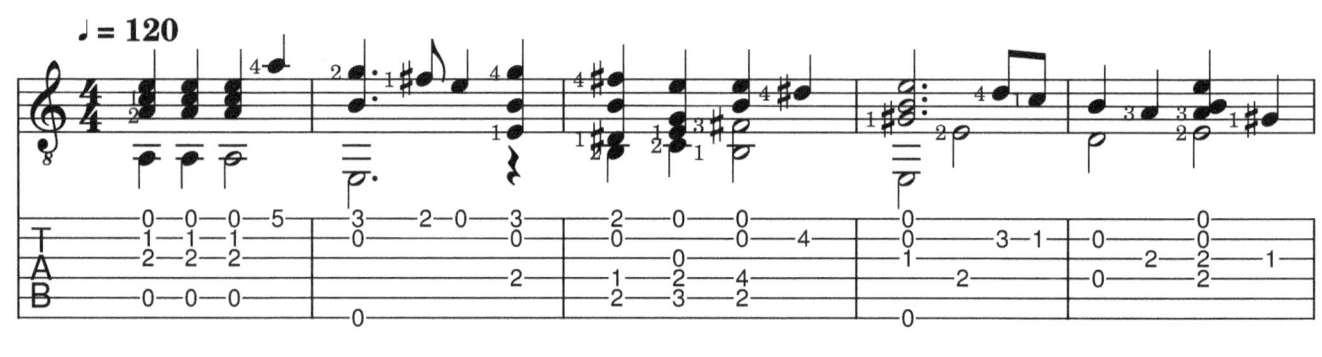

Toy

Francis Cutting (ca.1550-1595/1596)

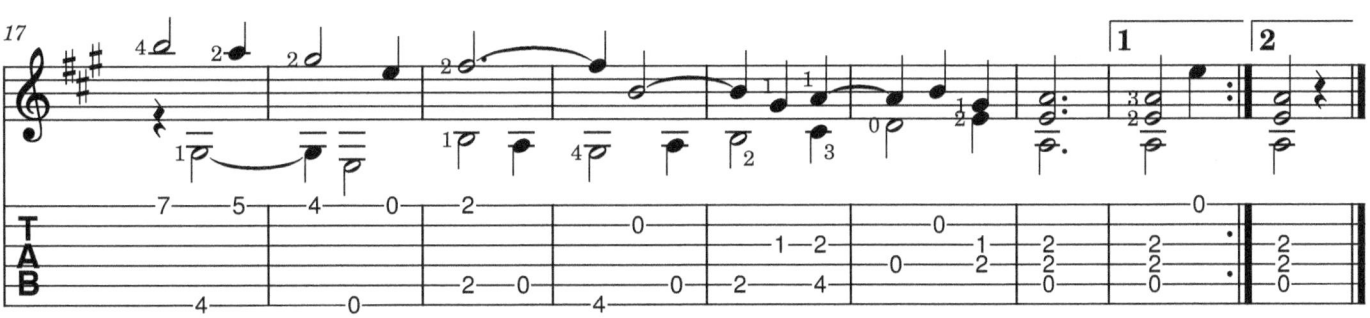

Packington's Pound

Francis Cutting
(ca.1550-1595/1596)

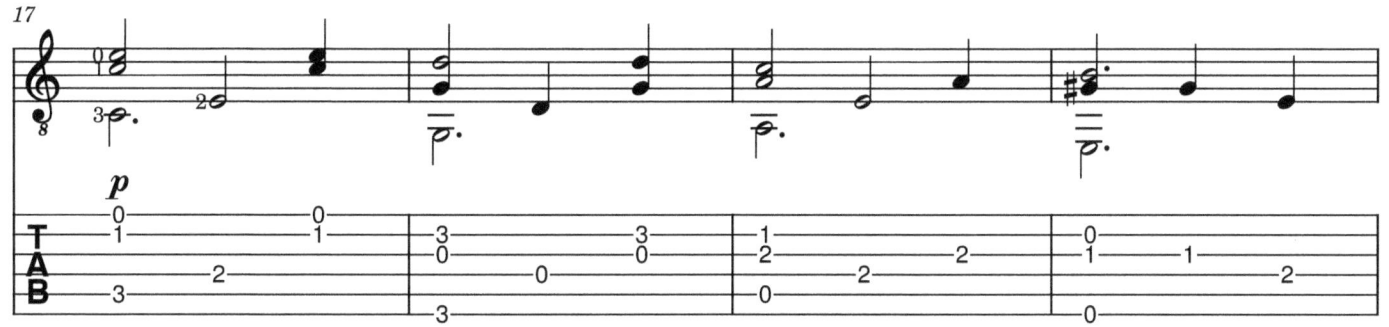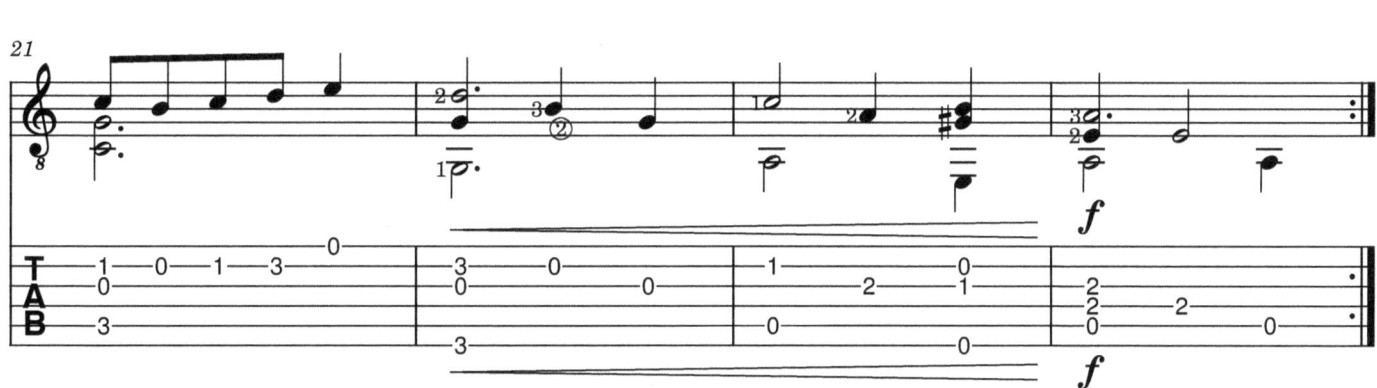

Mr. Dowland's Midnight

John Dowland (1563-1626)

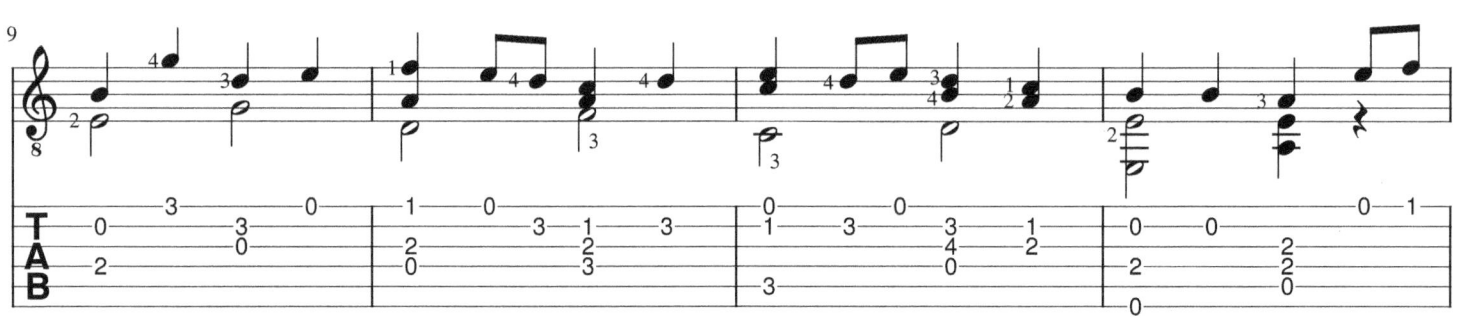

Orlando Sleepeth

John Dowland (1561-1626)

Baroque Composers

Henry Purcell (1659-1695)

Henry Purcell was an English organist and Baroque composer of secular and sacred music. Although Purcell incorporated Italian and French stylistic elements into his compositions, his legacy was a uniquely English form of Baroque music.

Gaspar Sanz (1640-1710)

Gaspar Sanz was an Aragonese composer, guitarist, organist and priest born to a wealthy family in Calanda in the Spanish comarca of Bajo Aragón. He studied music, theology and philosophy at the University of Salamanca, where he was later appointed Professor of Music.

Johann Krieger (1651-1735)

Krieger's keyboard music places him among the most important German composers of his time. The two published collections, Sechs musicalische Partien (1697) and Anmuthige Clavier-Übung (1698), contain harpsichord suites, organ toccatas, fugues, ricercars, and other works. Krieger's contemporaries praised his contrapuntal skill, evident in the extant fugues and ricercars. Johann Mattheson was particularly impressed with Krieger's double fugues, remarking that he knew nobody who surpassed Krieger in this form, except Handel. Handel himself admired and studied Krieger's work, even taking a copy of Anmuthige Clavier-Übung with him to England.

Johann Anton Logy (1645 – 1721)

Johann Anton Logy composed mostly dance suites. Losy mastered French **lute** style and his extant works demonstrate his intelligence, bright spirited love for the lute. His extensive and highly creative works are scattered through various archives

Johann Georg Leopold Mozart (1719 –1787)

Johann Georg Leopold Mozart was a German composer, conductor, teacher, and violinist. Mozart is best known today as the father and teacher of Wolfgang Amadeus Mozart, and for his violin textbook Versuch.

Robert de Visee (1655 – 1732)

Robert de Visée was a lutenist, guitarist, theorbist and viol player at the court of Louis XIV, as well as a singer, and composer for lute, theorbo and guitar. Robert de Visée's origin is unknown, although a Portuguese origin of his surname had been suggested. Visée published two books of guitar music which contained twelve suites between them, as well as a few isolated pieces.

Silvius Leopold Weiss (1687-1750)

Silvius Leopold Weiss was a German composer and lutenist. Weiss was one of the most important and most prolific composers of lute music in history and one of the best-known and most technically accomplished lutenists of his day. He wrote around 600 pieces for lute, most of them grouped into 'sonatas' or suites, which consist mostly of baroque dance pieces.

Johann Sebastian Bach (1685-1750)

Johann Sebastian Bach was a German composer, organist, harpsichordist, violist, and violinist whose sacred and secular works for choir, orchestra, and solo instruments drew together the strands of the Baroque period and brought it to its ultimate maturity.

Giuseppe Antonio Brescianello (1690-1758)

Giuseppe Antonio Brescianello was an Italian Baroque composer and violinist. He invigorated musical life in Stuttgart. His contemporaries praised his chamber works. The music of Brescianello shows great sense of melody, profound harmonic imagination combined with strong rhythmic element so typical to Italian school of the time.

Aria

Henry Purcell (1659 - 1695)

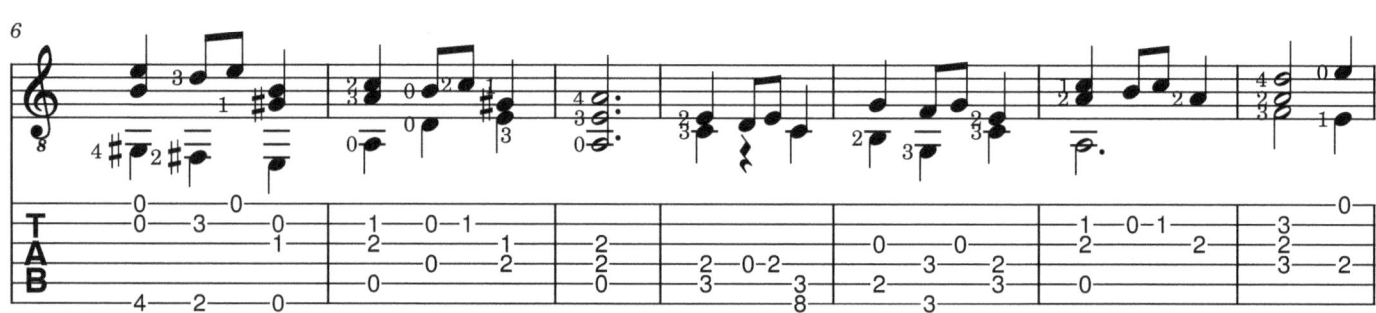

Paradetas

Gaspar Sanz (1640-1710)

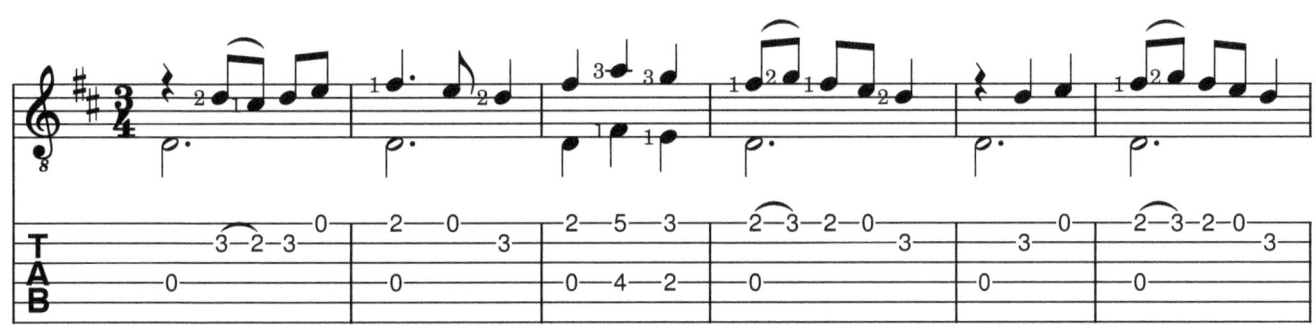

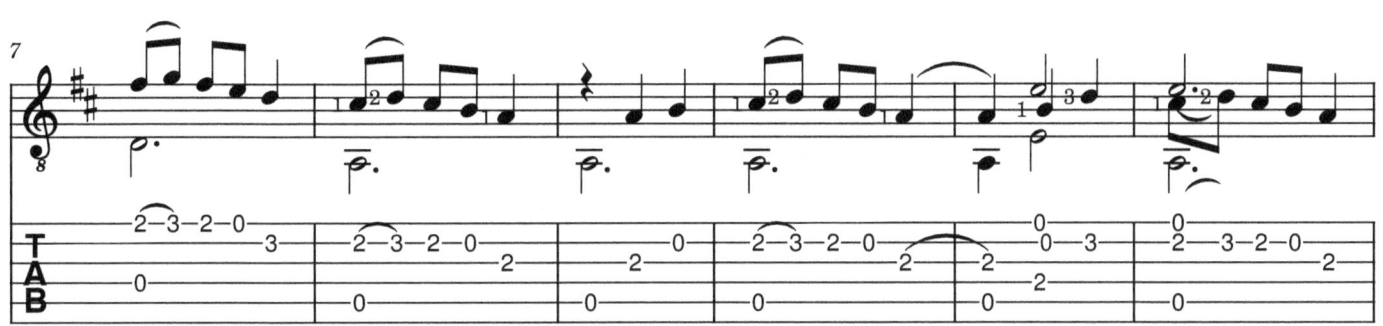

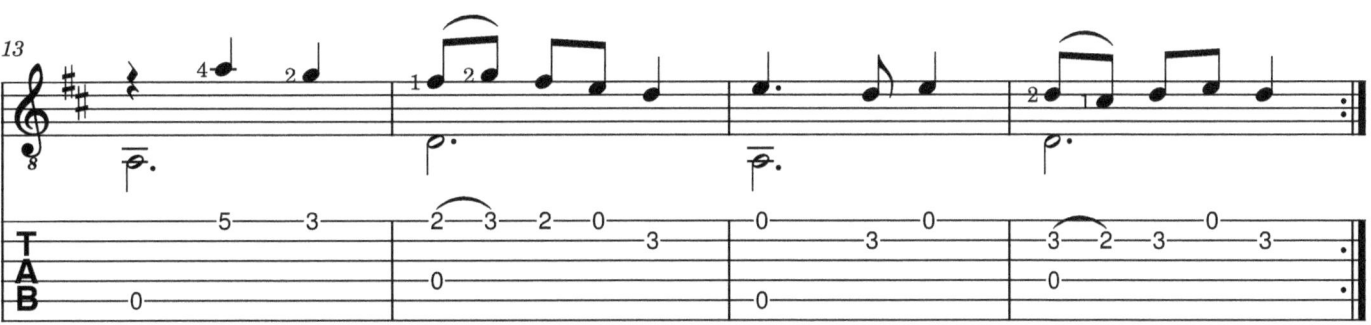

Rujero

Gaspar Sanz (1640-1710)

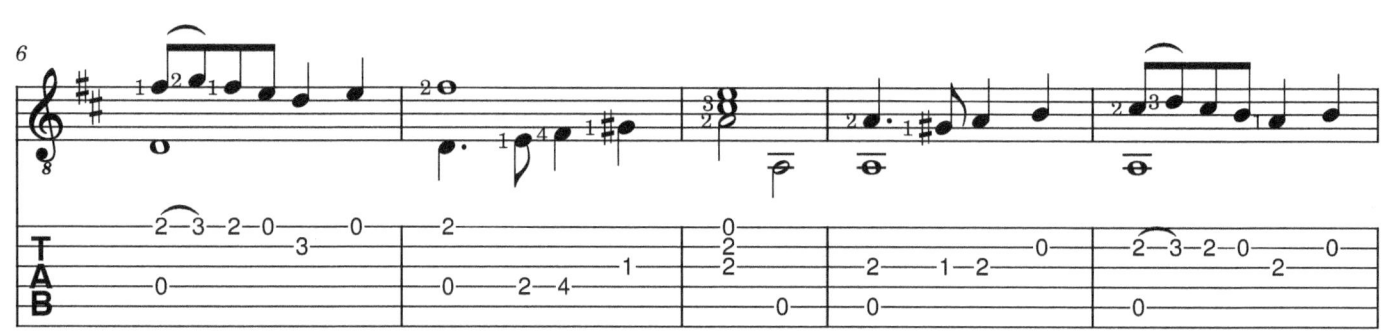

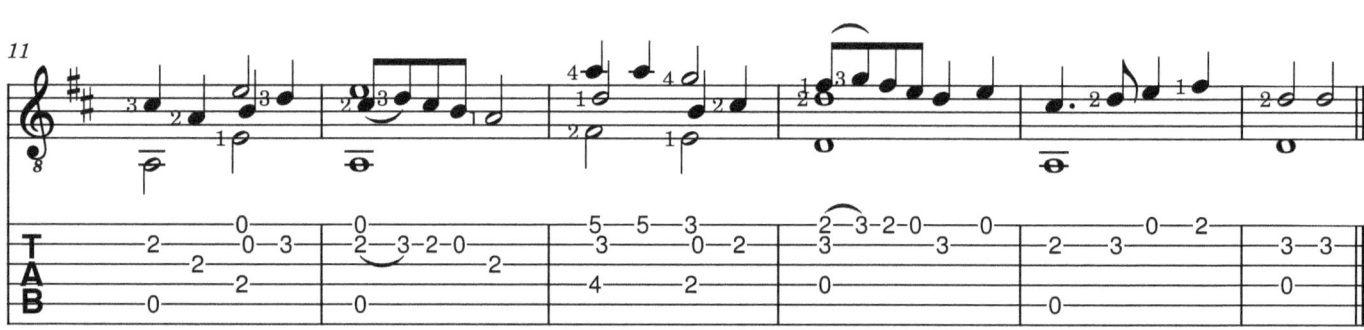

Bourrée

Johann Krieger (1651–1735)

Gigue

Johann Anton Logy (1650 - 1721)

Bourree

Leopold Mozart (1719-1787)

Menuet

Johann Christoph Friederich Bach (1732-1795)

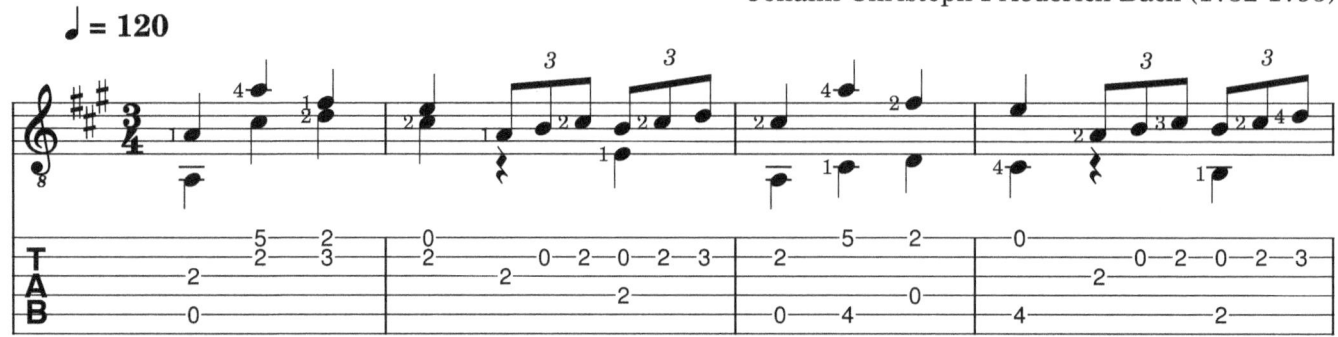
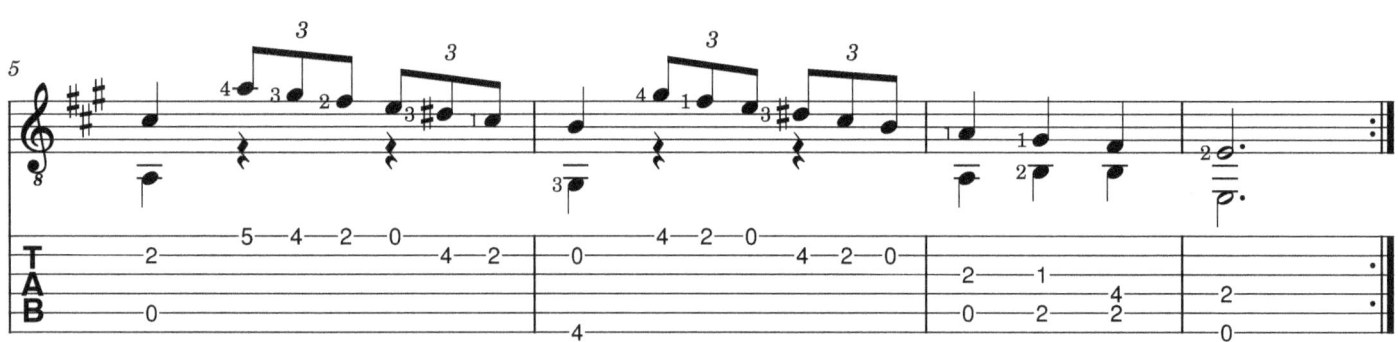
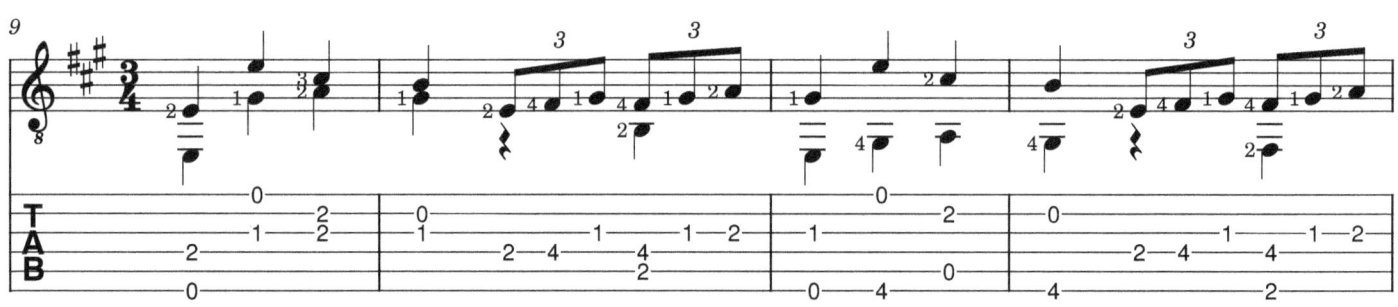

Menuet

Johann Krieger (1651–1735)

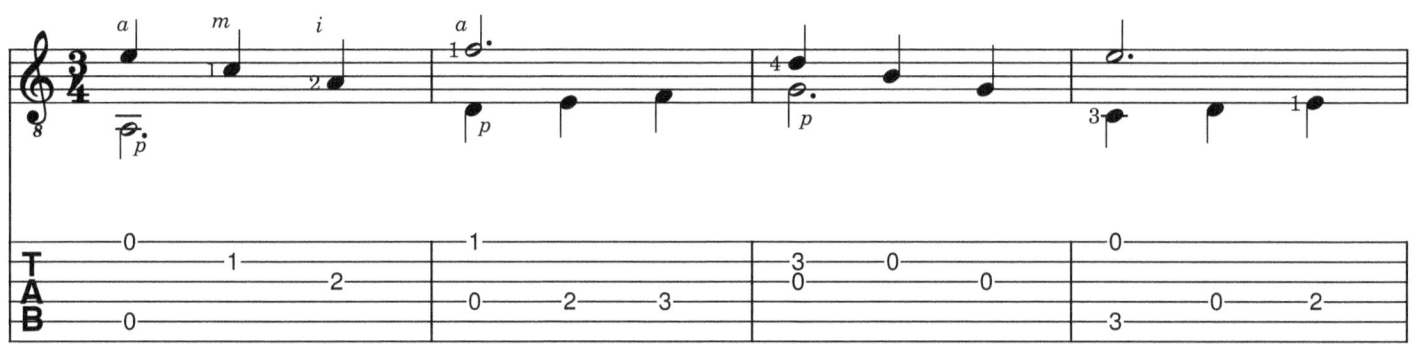
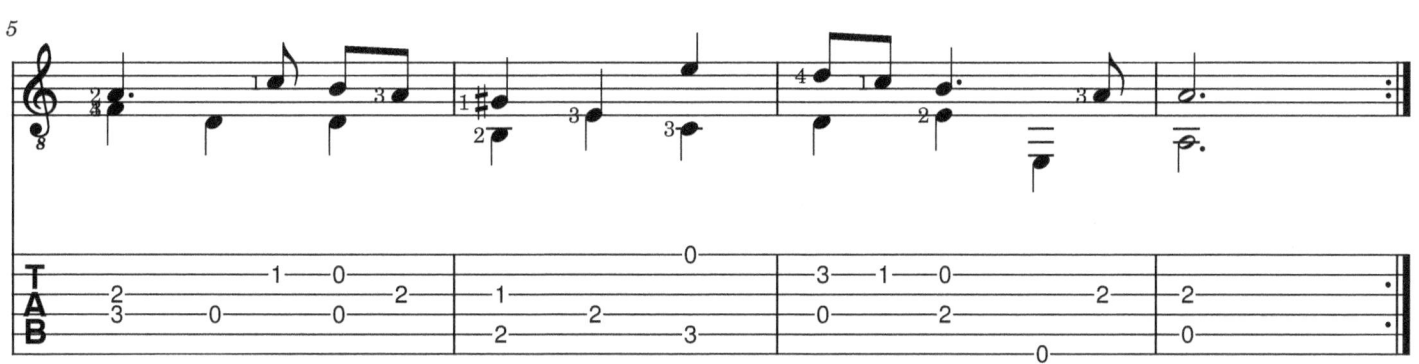
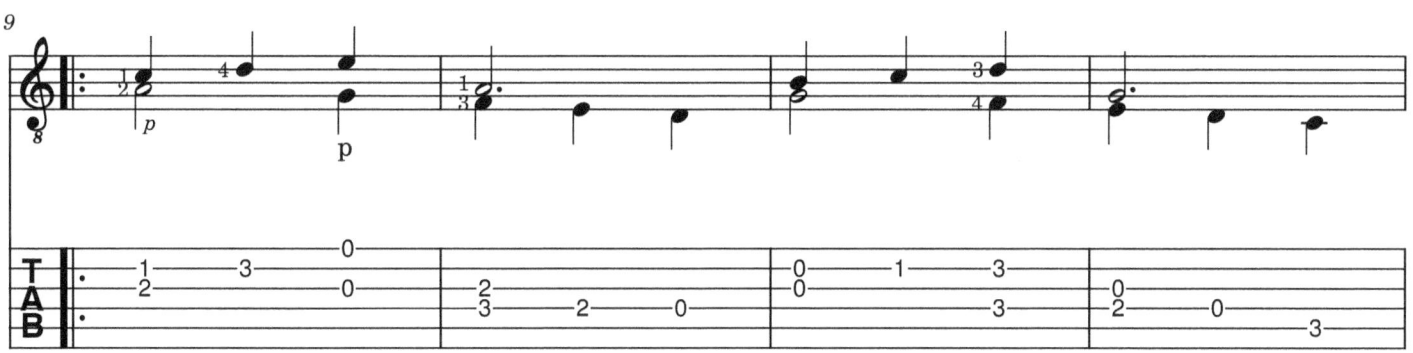
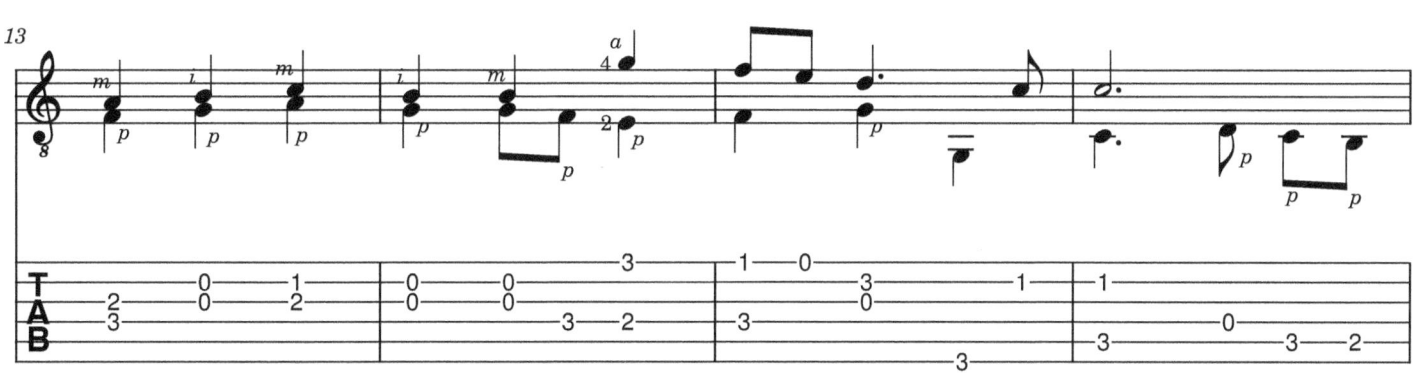

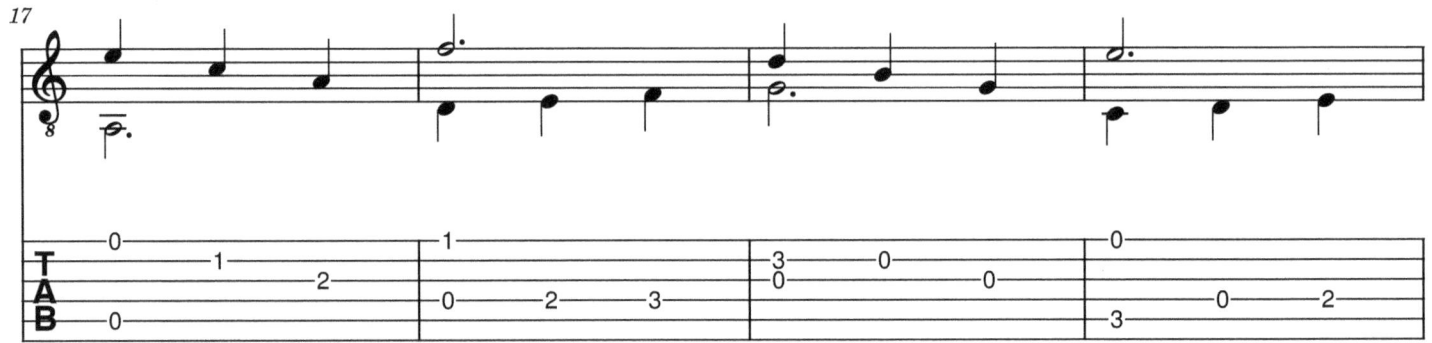
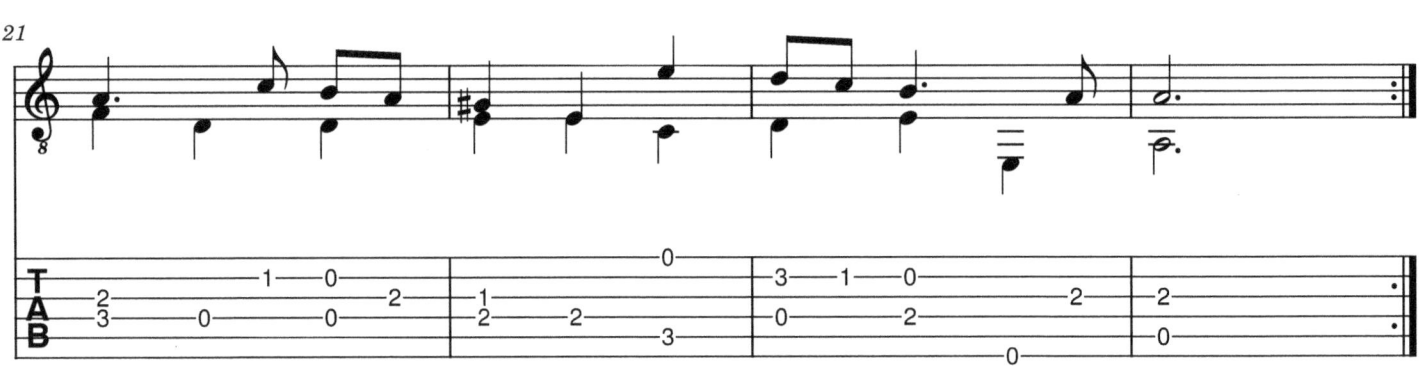

Menuet

Robert de Visée (1650-1725)

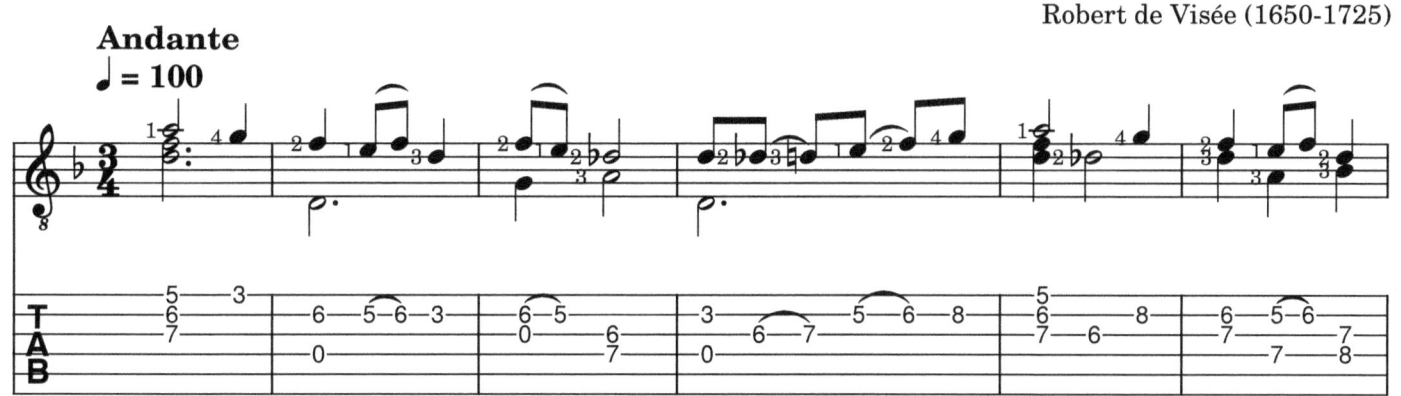
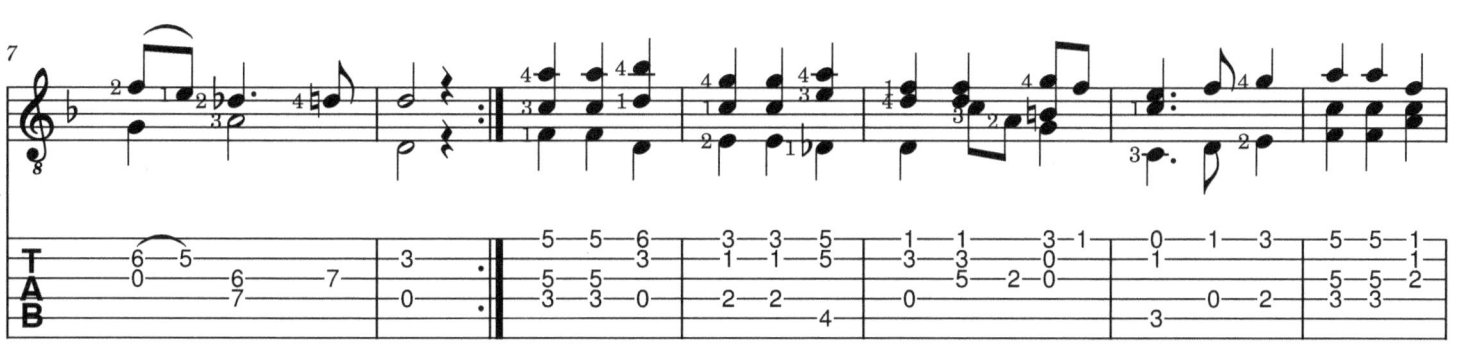

Menuet

Silvius Leopold Weiss (1687-1750)

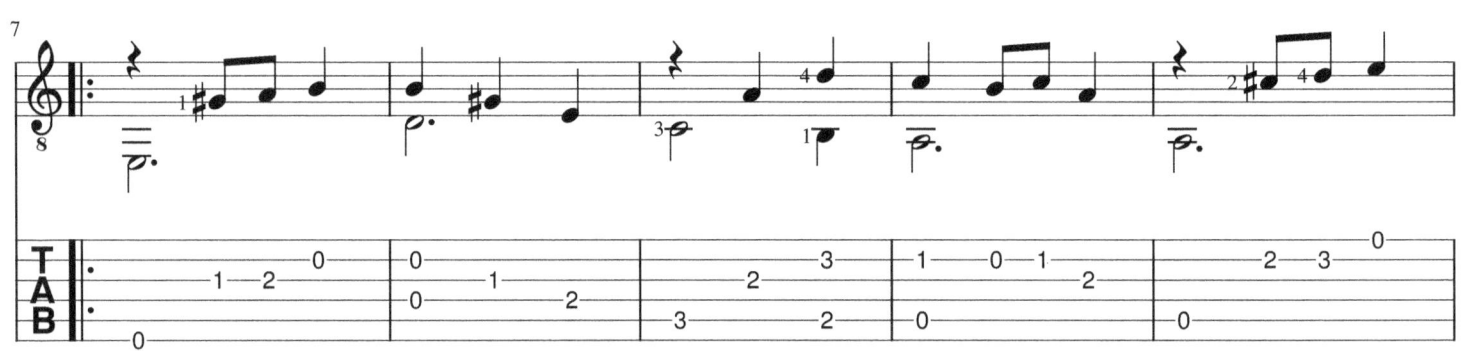
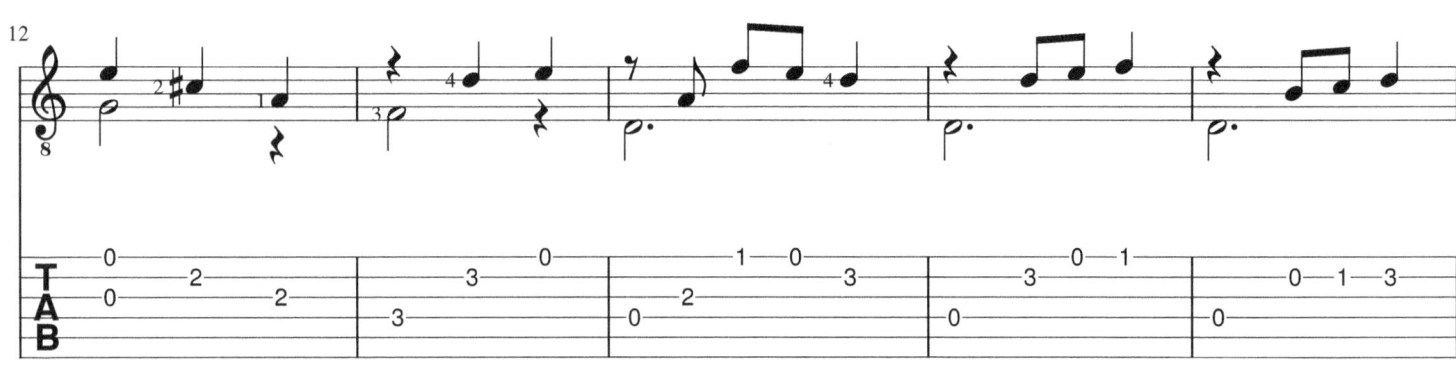

Españoleta

Gaspar Sanz (1640-1710)

Grazioso ♩ = 120

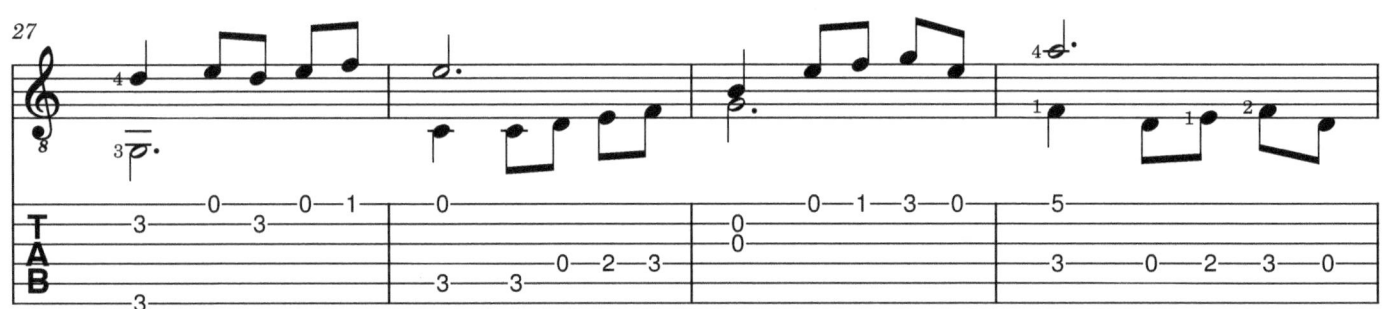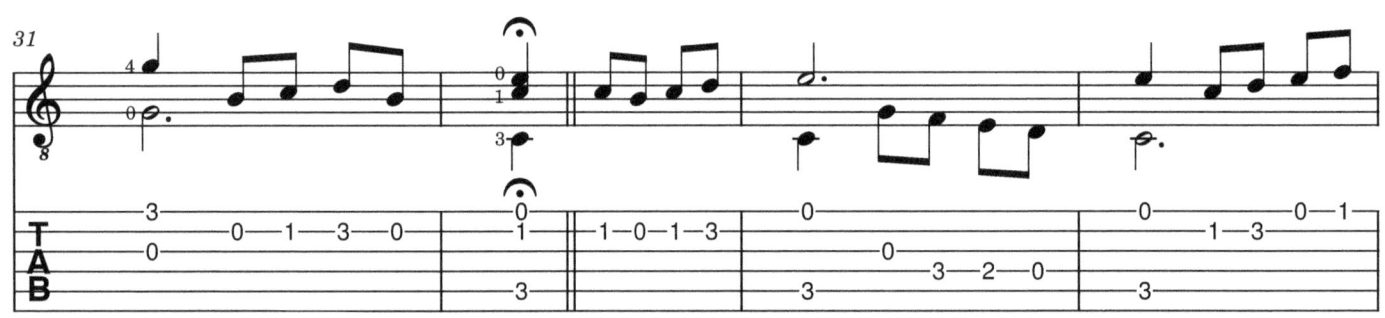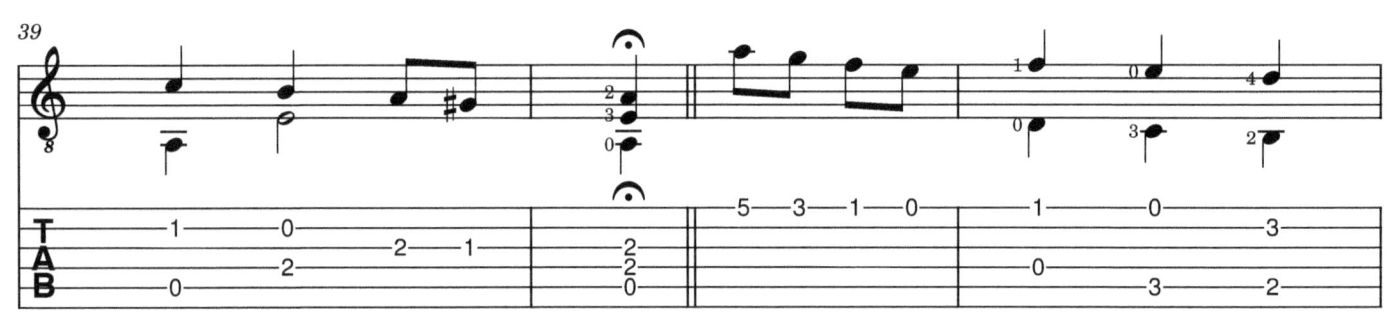

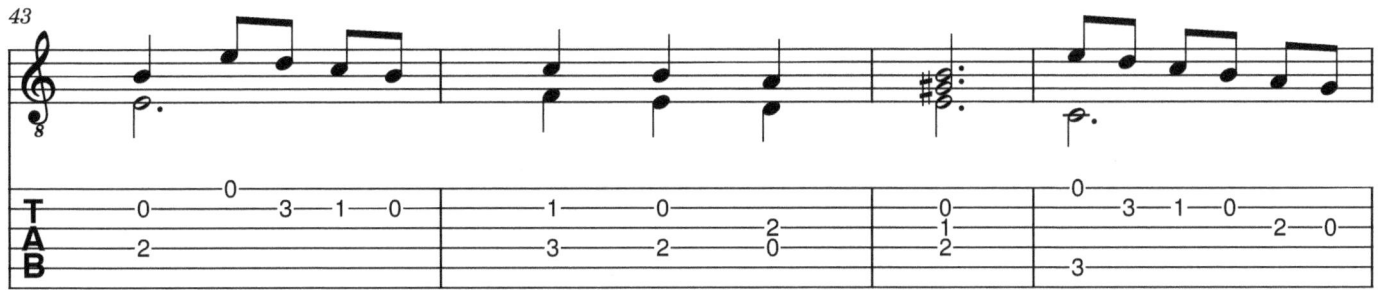
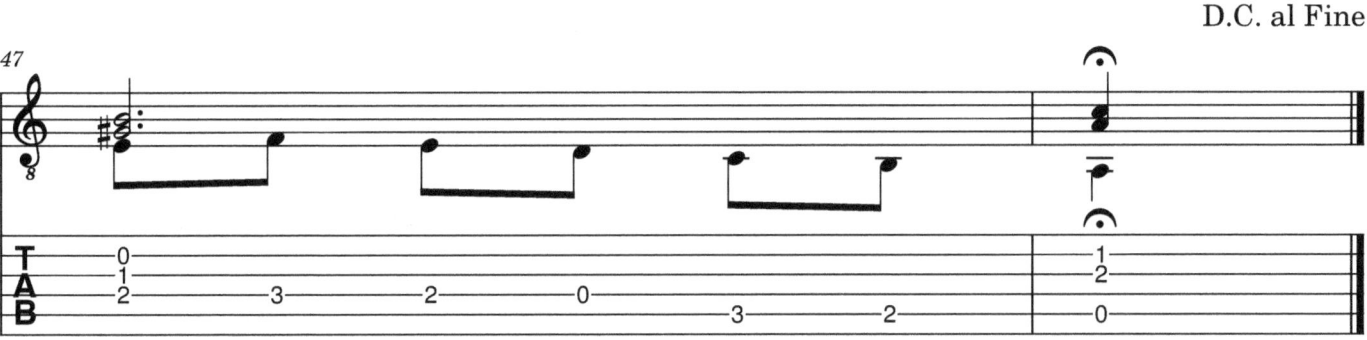

D.C. al Fine

Menuet in G

Johann Sebastian Bach (1685-1750) BWV Anh. 114

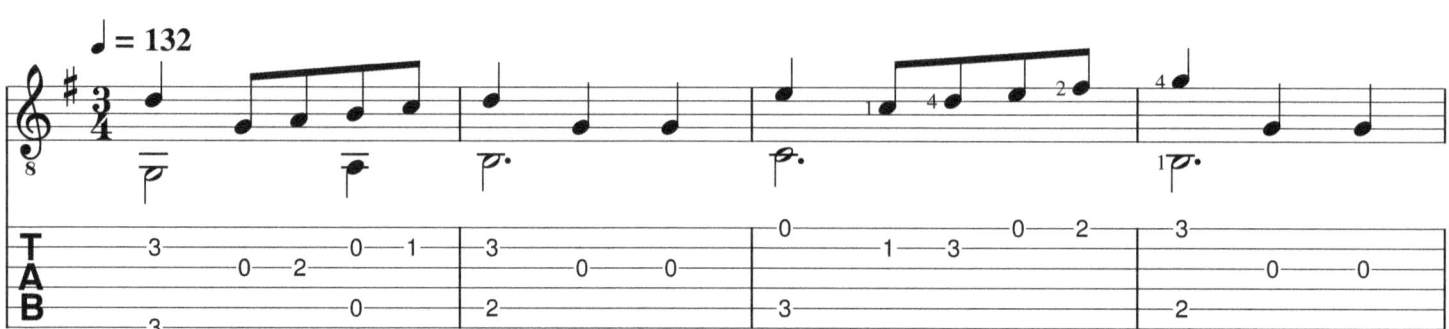

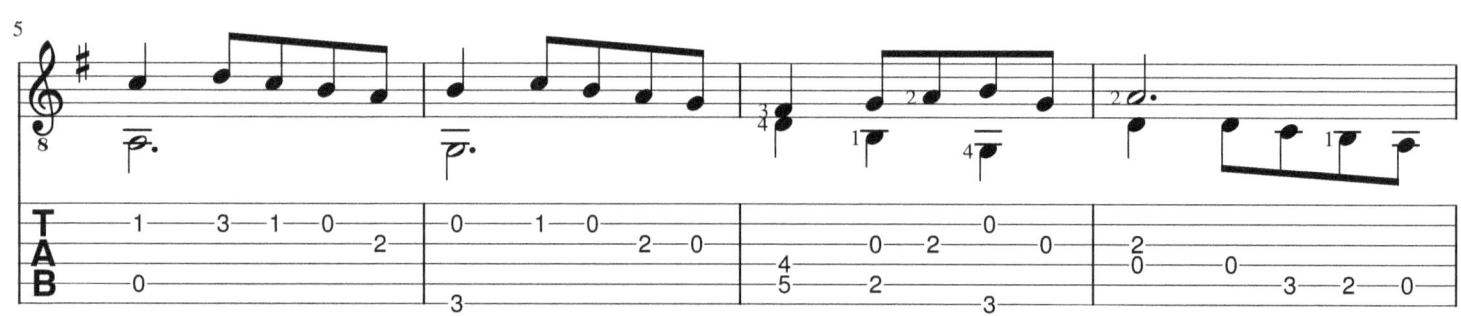

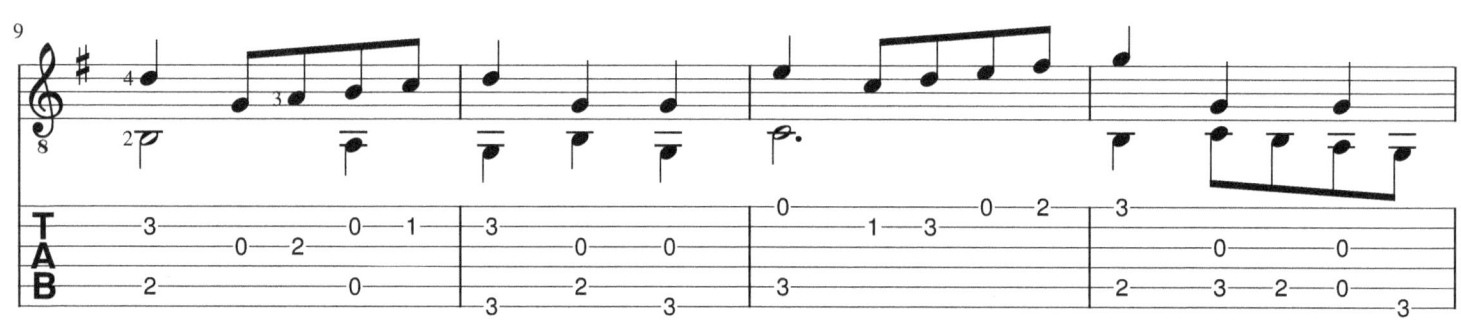

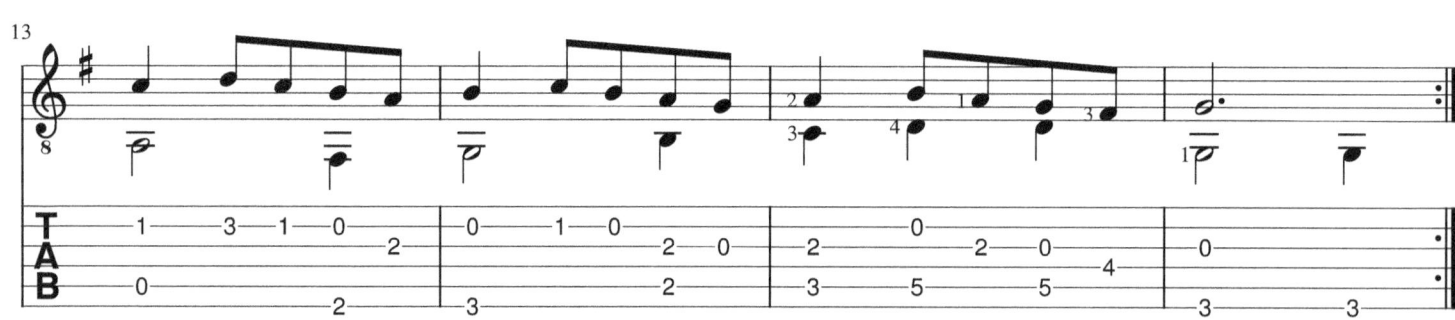

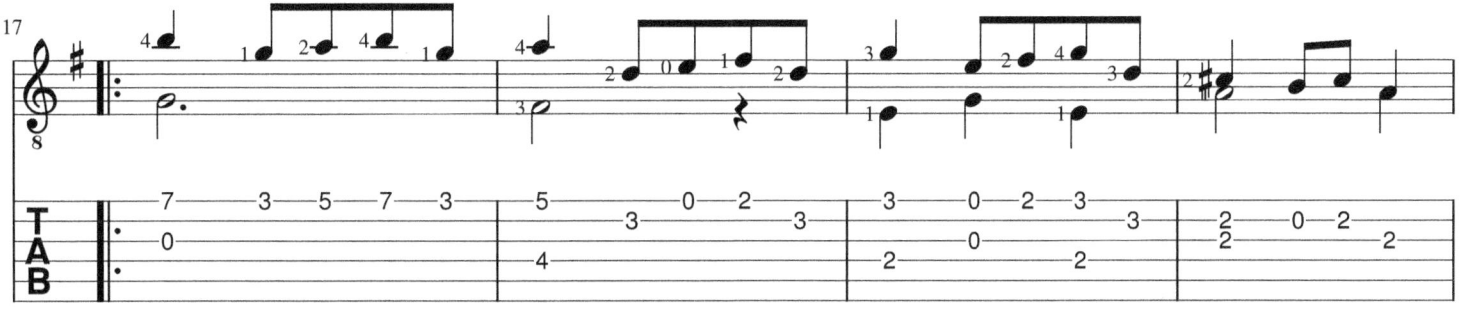
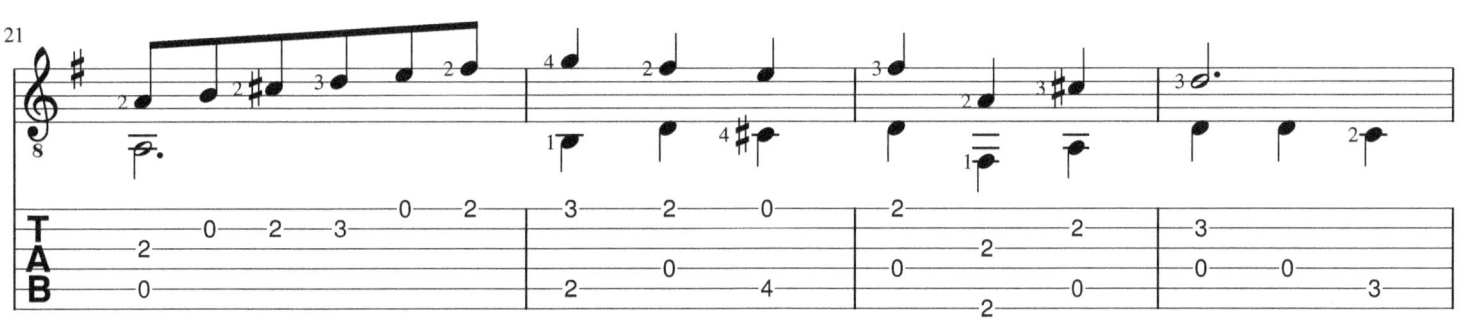

Gigue

Giuseppe Antonio Brescianello (1690-1758)

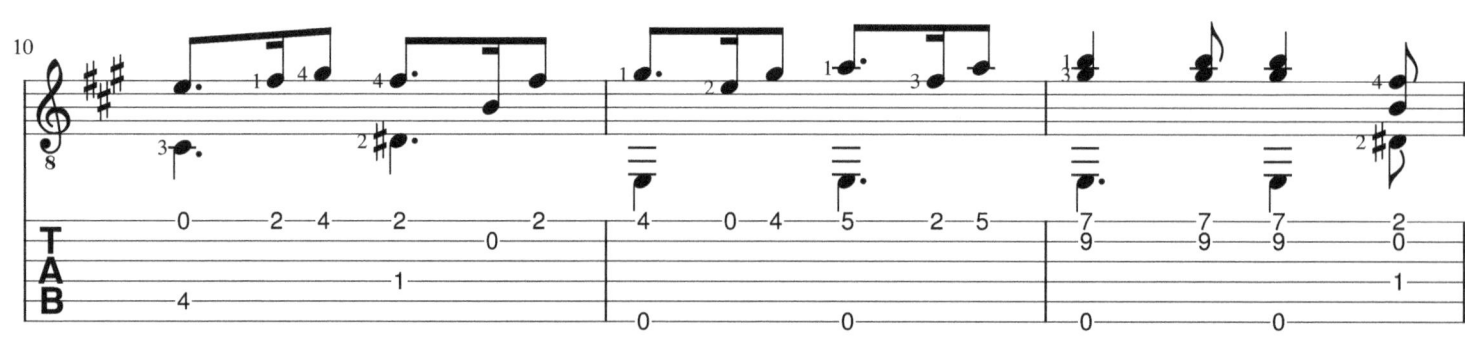

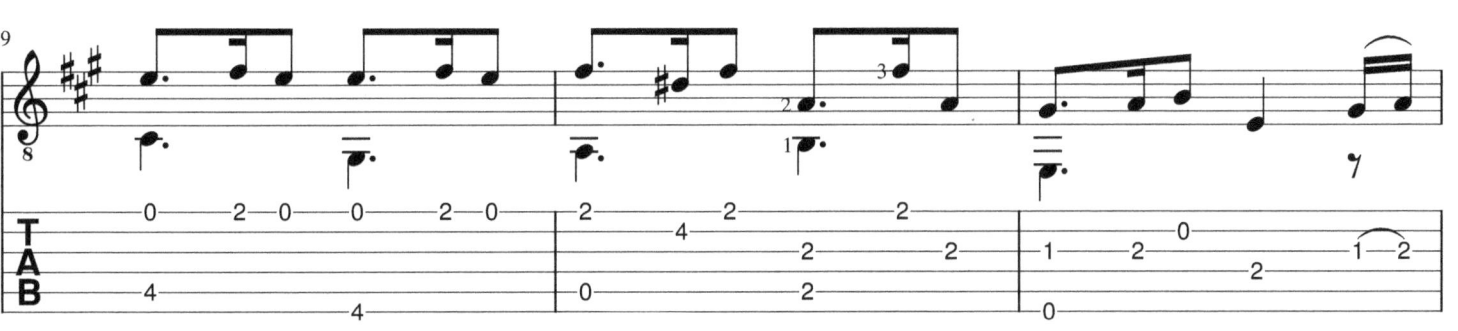

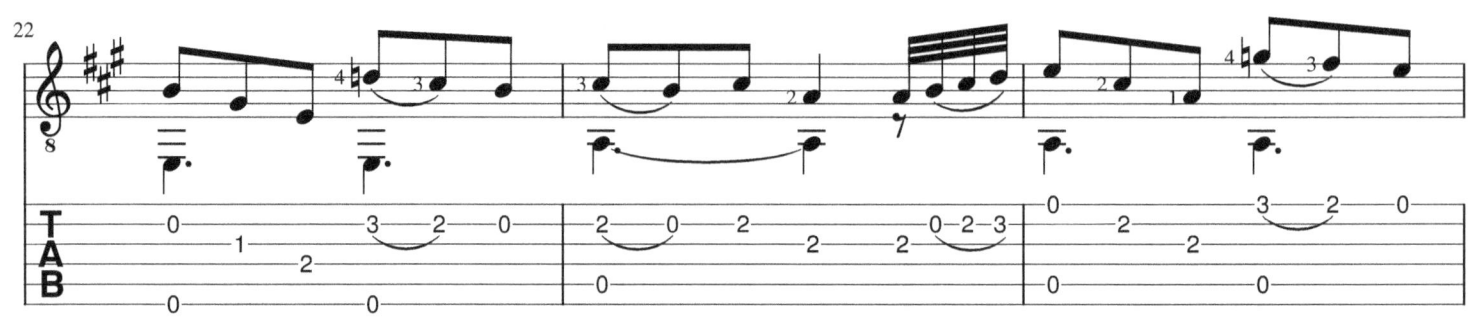
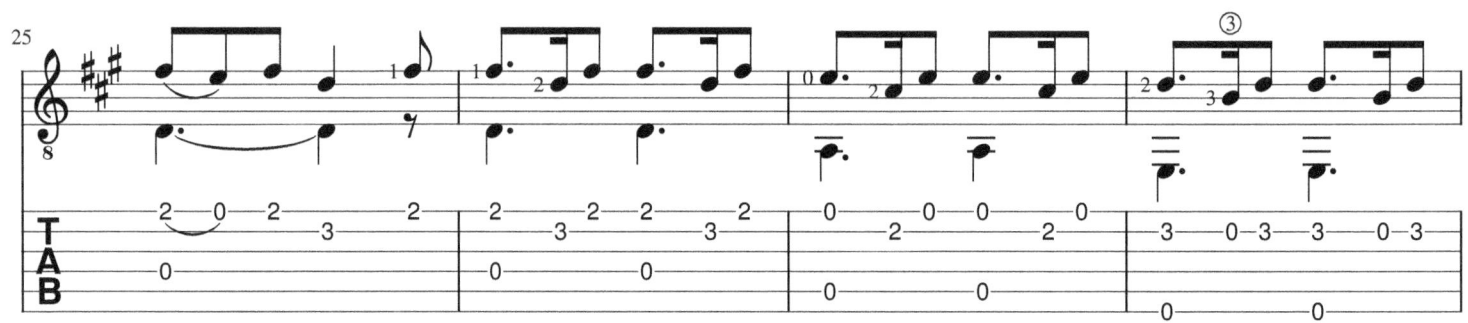

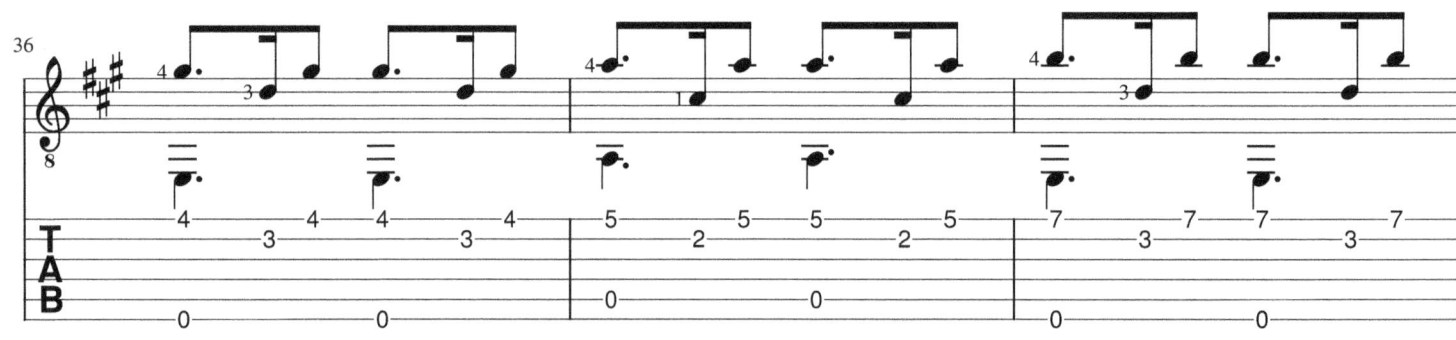

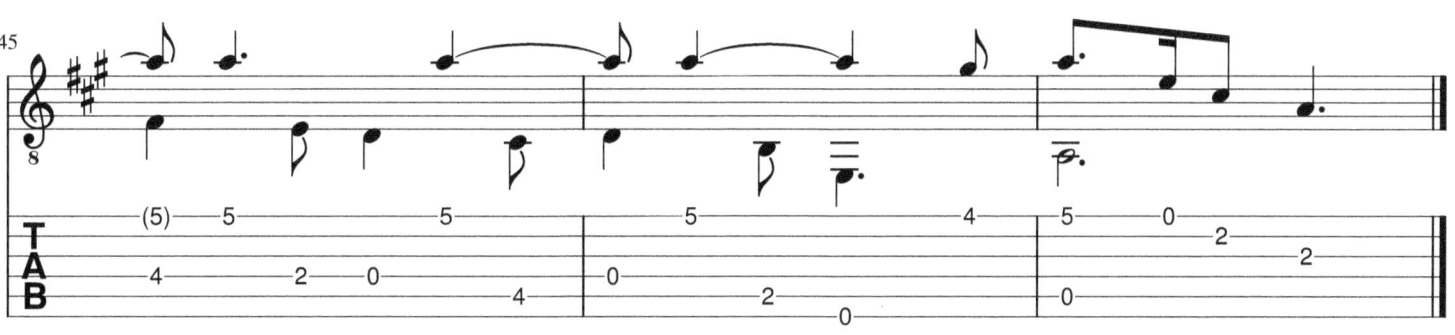

Bourrée - Suite in D minor

Robert de Visée (1650-1725)

Classical Era Composers

Ferdinando Carulli (1770-1841)

Ferdinando Carulli was born in Naples, Italy on February 10, 1770. Carulli's first musical instruction was on the cello, but he soon turned his attention to the guitar. Carulli was entirely self taught, as there were no guitar teachers in Naples at the time. Despite having no formal instruction on the guitar, Carulli rapidly became known as one of the leading virtuosos of his day.

Fernando Sor (1778-1839)

Fernando Sor was a Spanish classical guitarist and composer. He is best known for his guitar compositions, but he also composed music for opera and ballet, earning acclaim for his ballet titled Cendrillon. Sor's works for guitar range from pieces for advanced players, such as Variations on a Theme of Mozart, to beginner pieces.

Mauro Giuliani (1781-1829)

Mauro Giuliani was an italian guitarist and composer, and is considered by many to be one of the leading guitarist virtuosos of the early nineteenth century. He was a prolific composer, writing over 150 pieces for the guitar, as well as many chamber compositions for the violin, voice, flute, piano, and chamber orchestra.

Dionisio Aguado (1784-1849)

Dionisio Aguado was a Spanish classical guitarist and composer. Born in Madrid, he studied with Miguel Garcia. In 1825, Aguado visited Paris, where he met and became friends with lived with Fernando Sor. Aguado's major work Escuela de Guitarra was a guitar tutorial published in 1825. Dionisio Aguado has attained lasting fame through his method for guitar, which is still in print today.

Anton Diabelli (1781-1858)

Anton (or Antonio) Diabelli was an Austrian music publisher, editor and composer of Italian descent. Best known in his time as a publisher, he is most familiar today as the composer of the waltz on which Ludwig van Beethoven wrote his set of thirty-three Diabelli Variations.

Andante (1)

Ferdinando Carulli

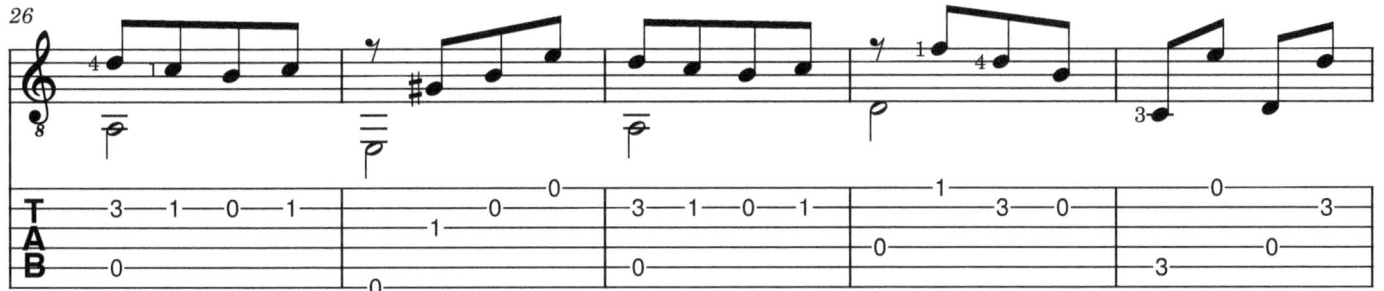

Andante (1) in C

Fernando Sor (1778-1839)

Andante (2)

Fernando Sor (1778-1839)

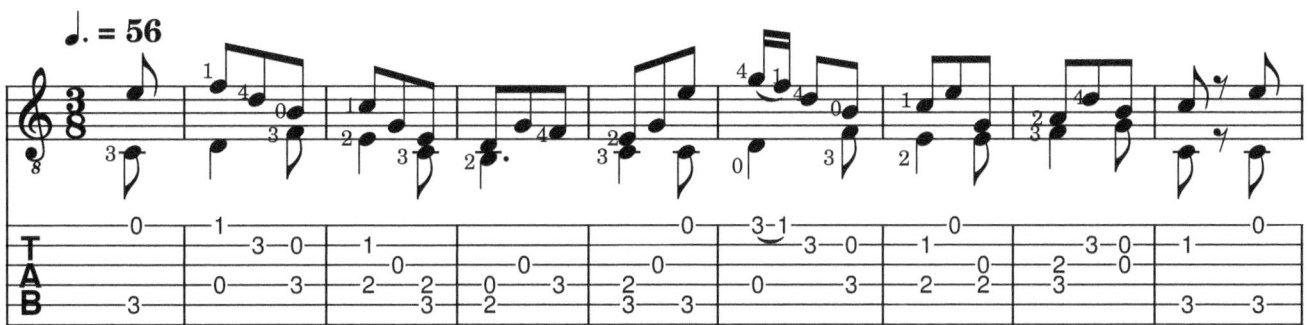
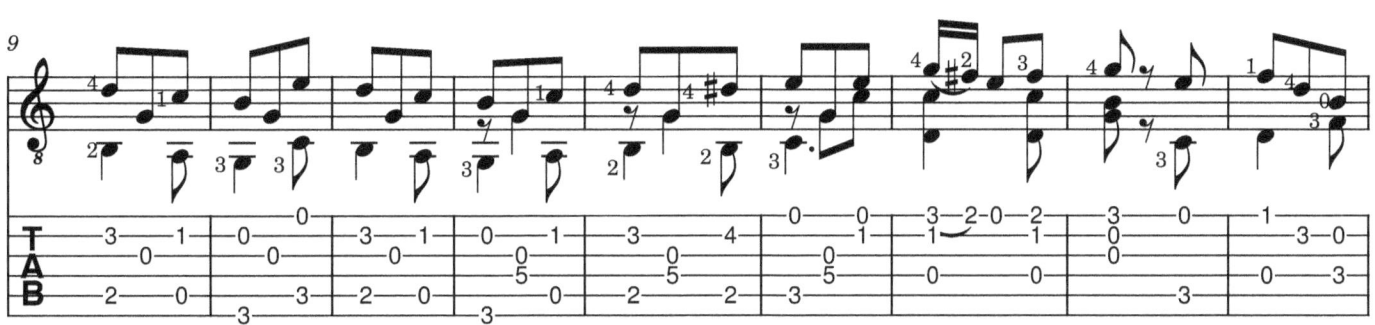
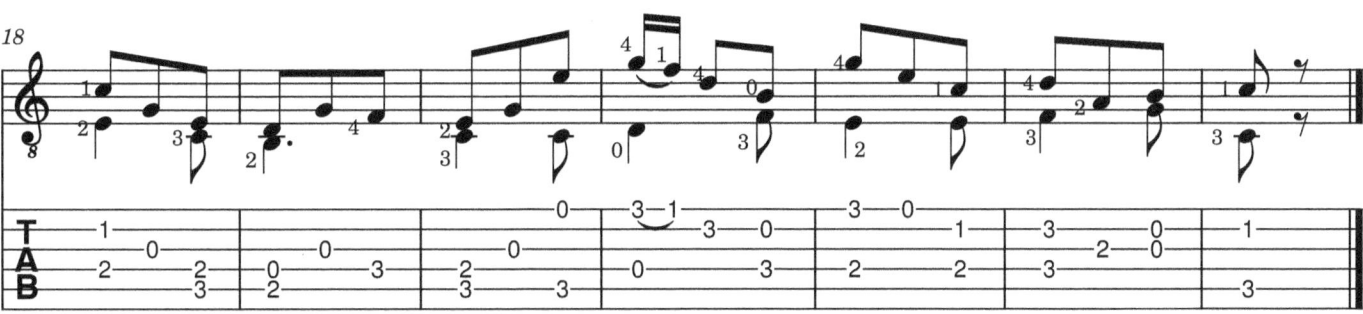

Andantino (1)

Ferdinando Carulli 1770-1841)

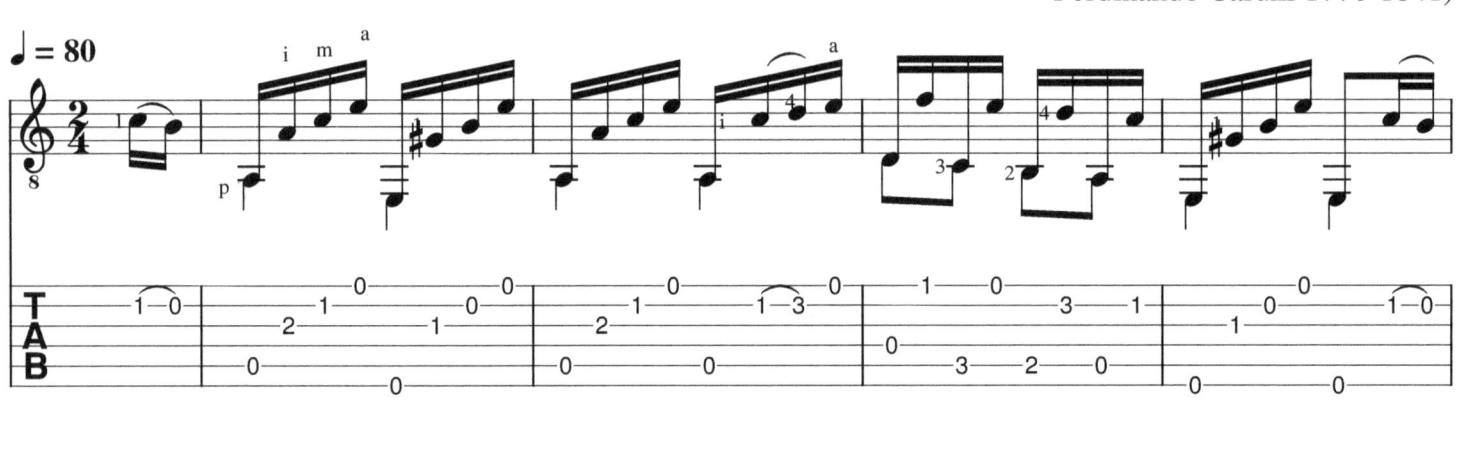
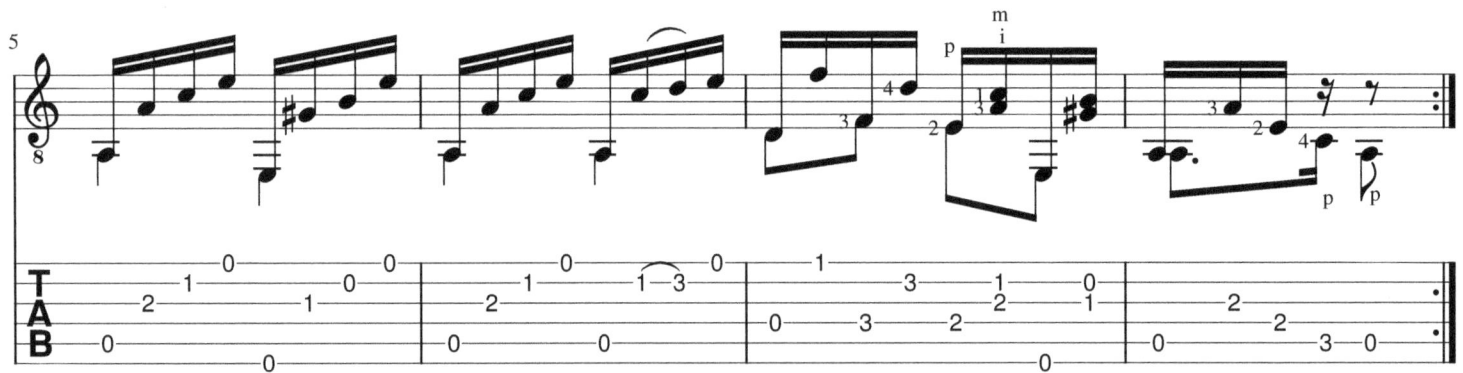
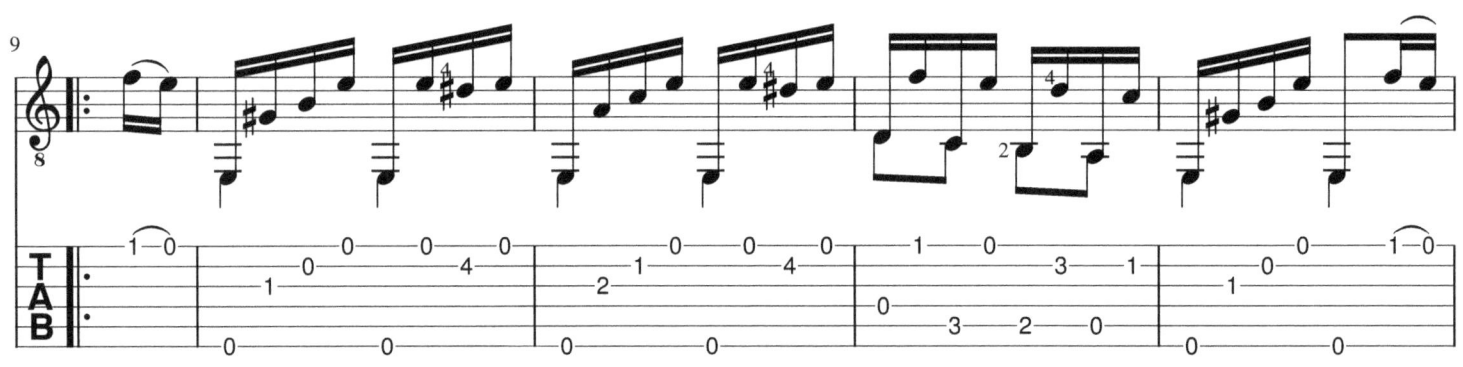
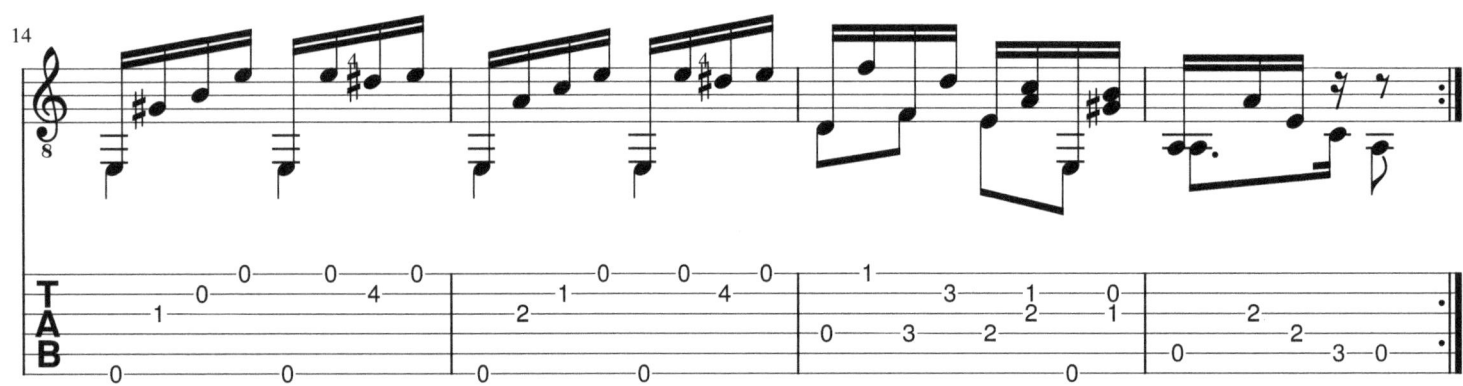

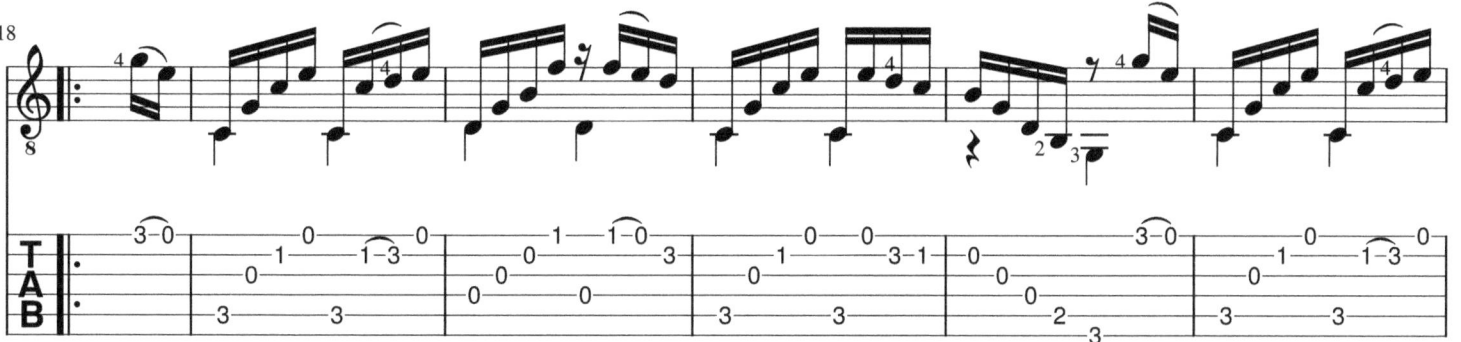

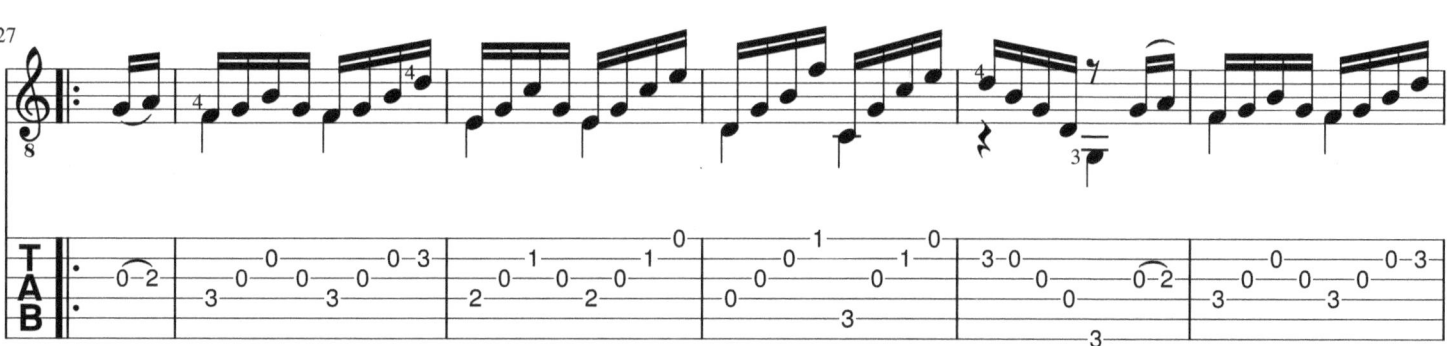
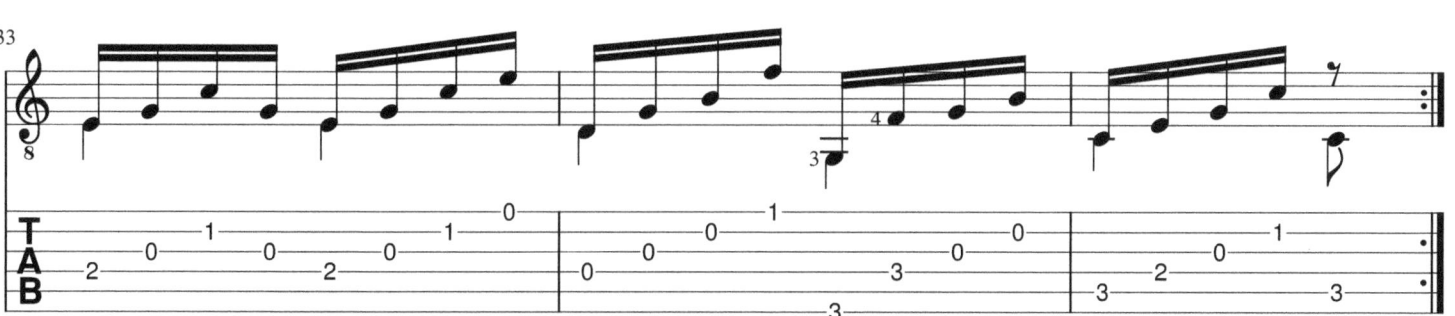

Andantino (2)

Ferdinando Carulli (1770-1841)

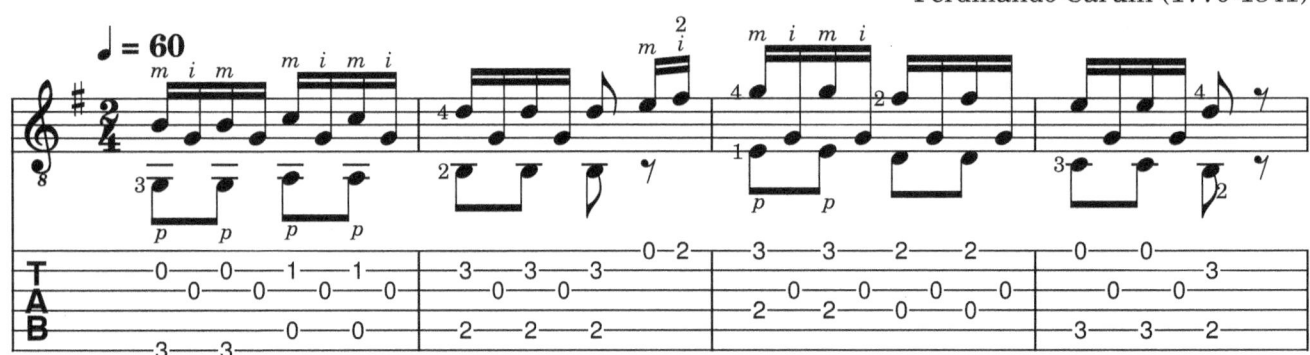
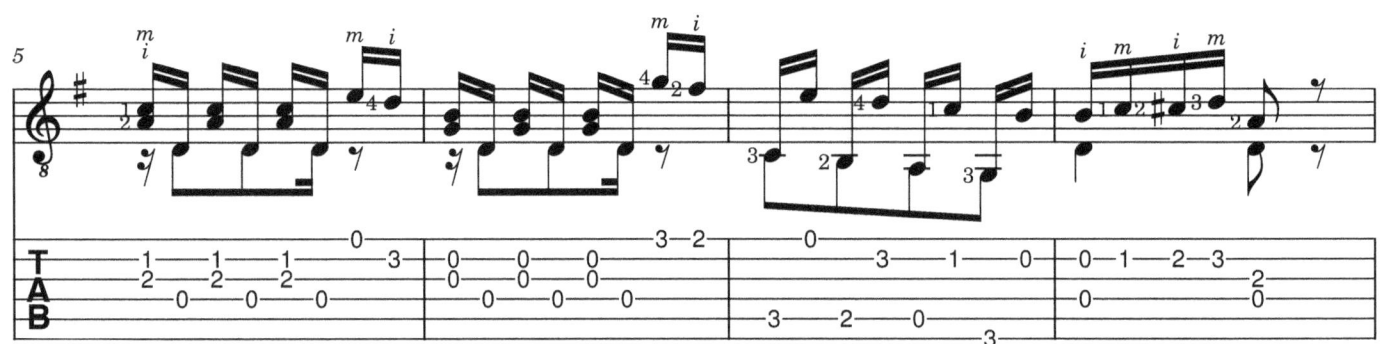
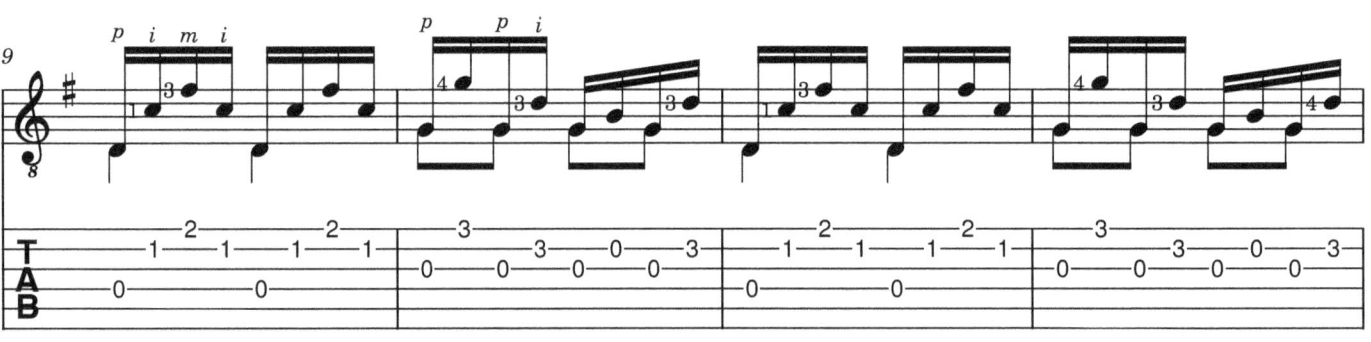
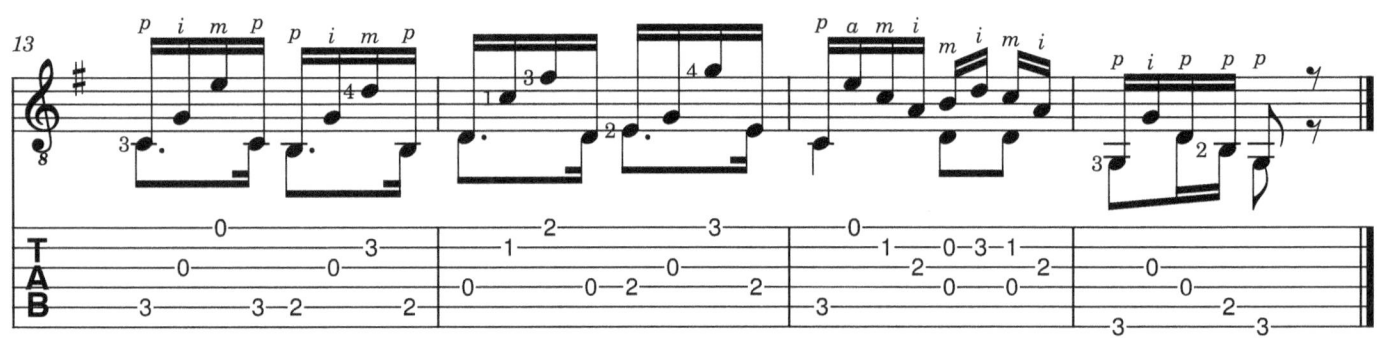

Ecossaise

Mauro Giuliani

Allegretto ♩ = 88

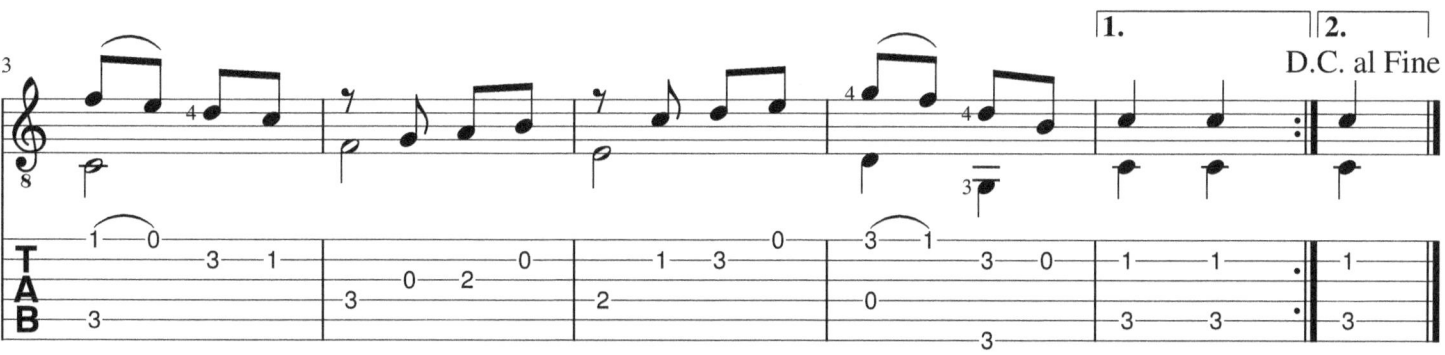

Allegro

Mauro Giuliani (1781-1829)

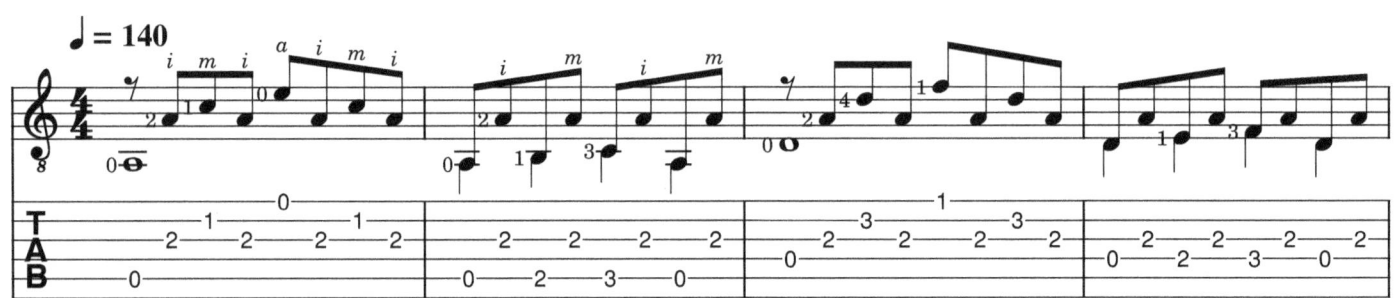
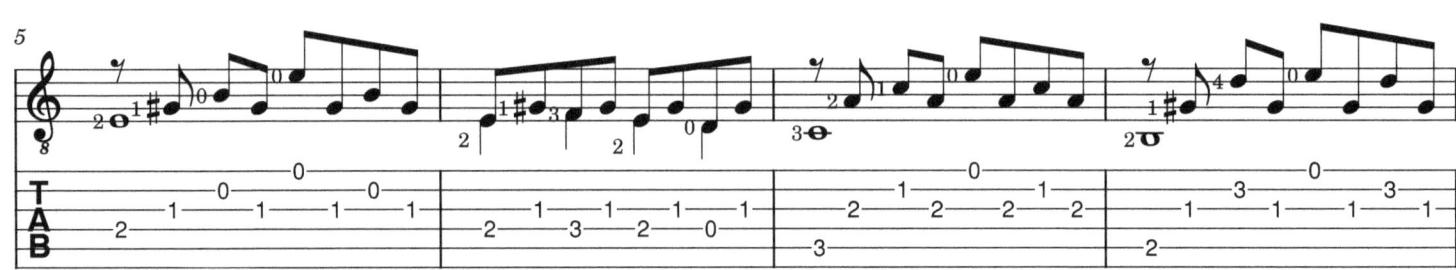
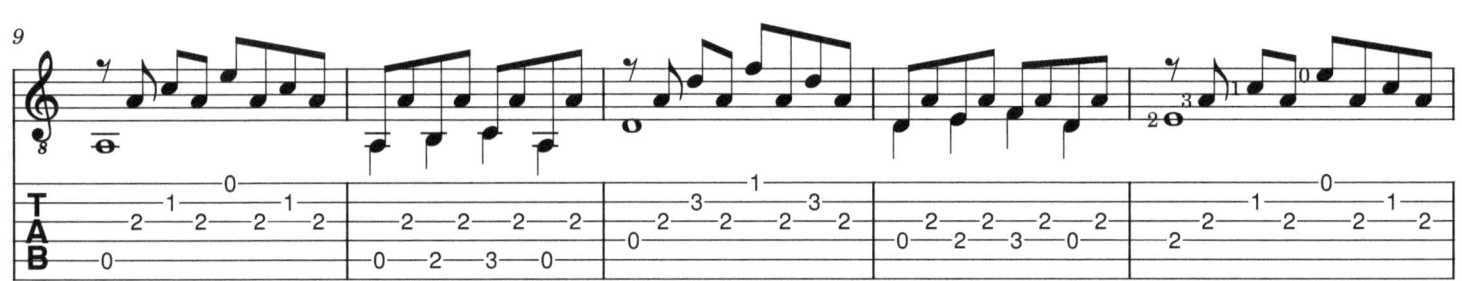
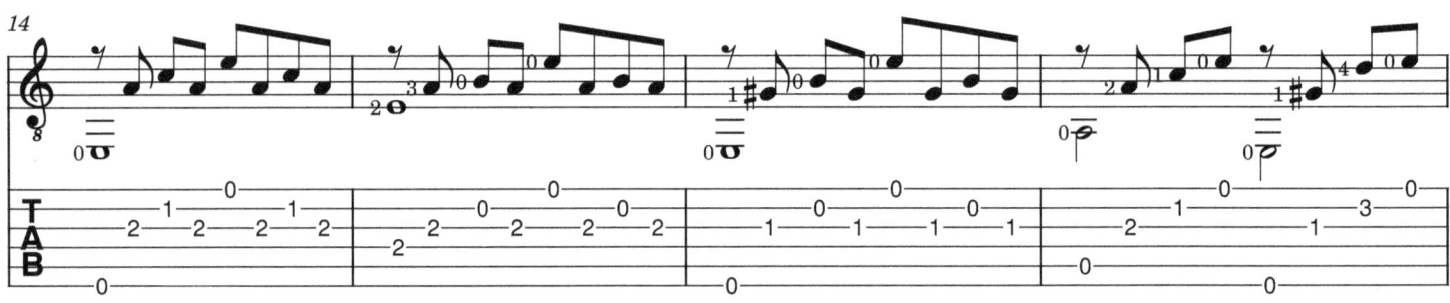
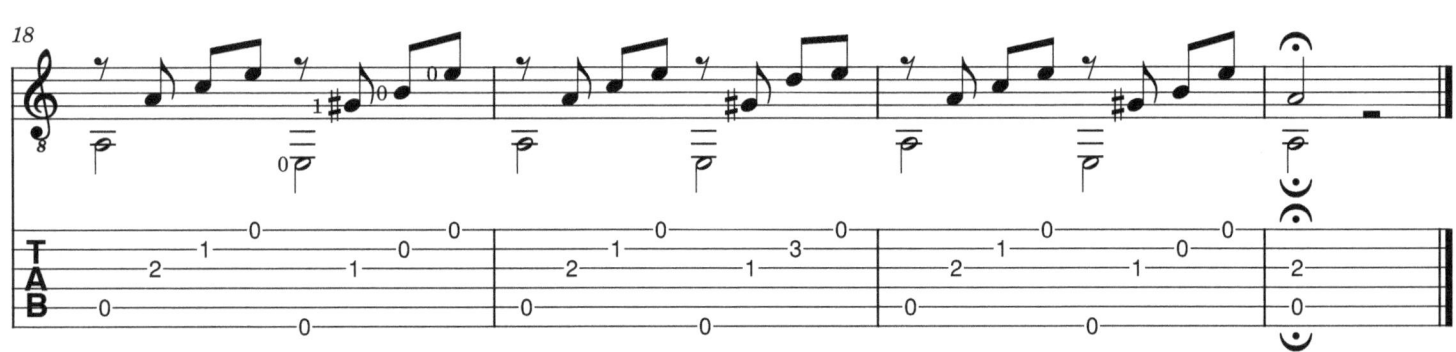

Etude A minor

Dionisio AGUADO (1784-1849)

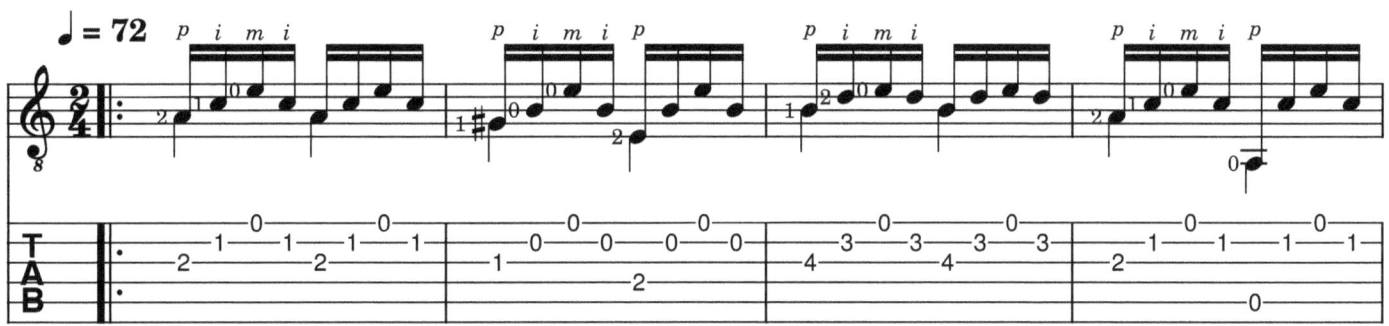
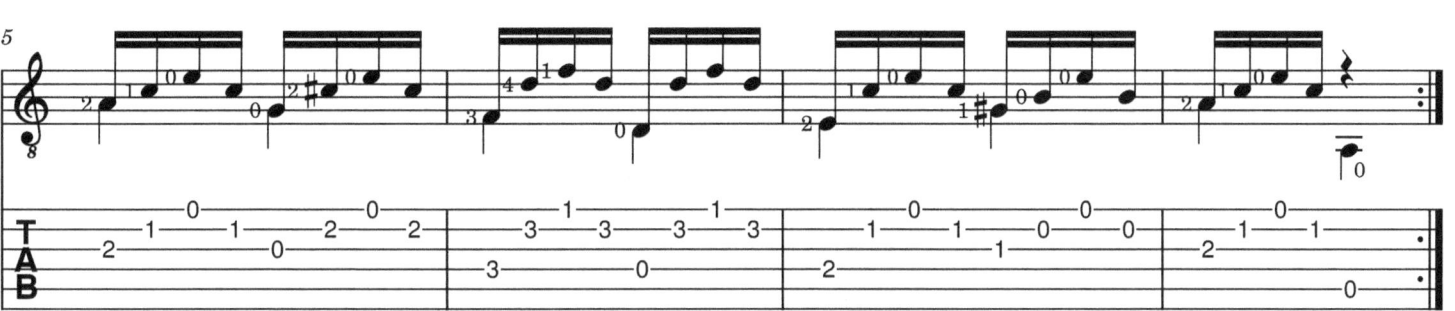

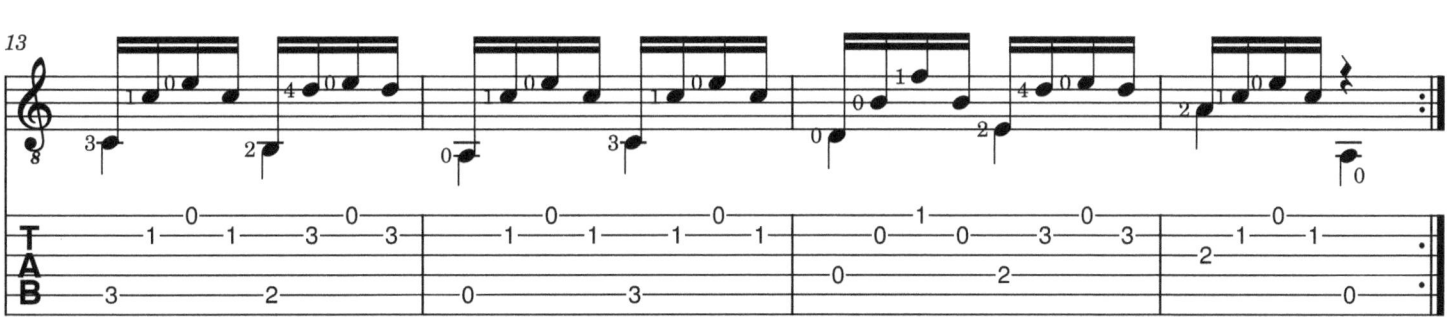

Menuet in A minor

Dionisio Aguado (1784 - 1849)

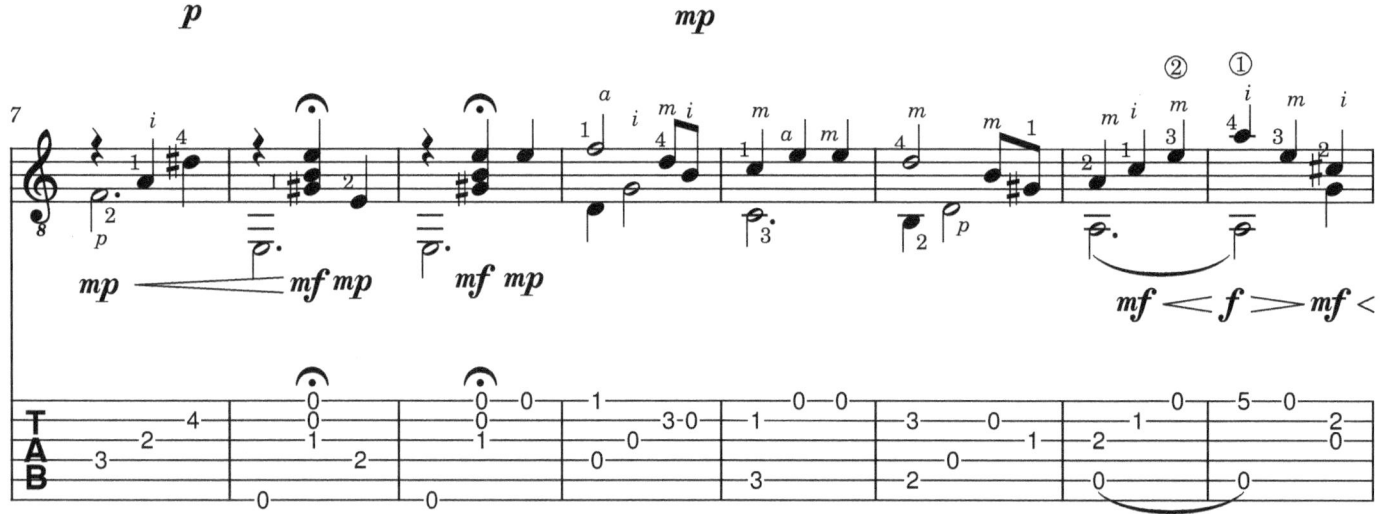
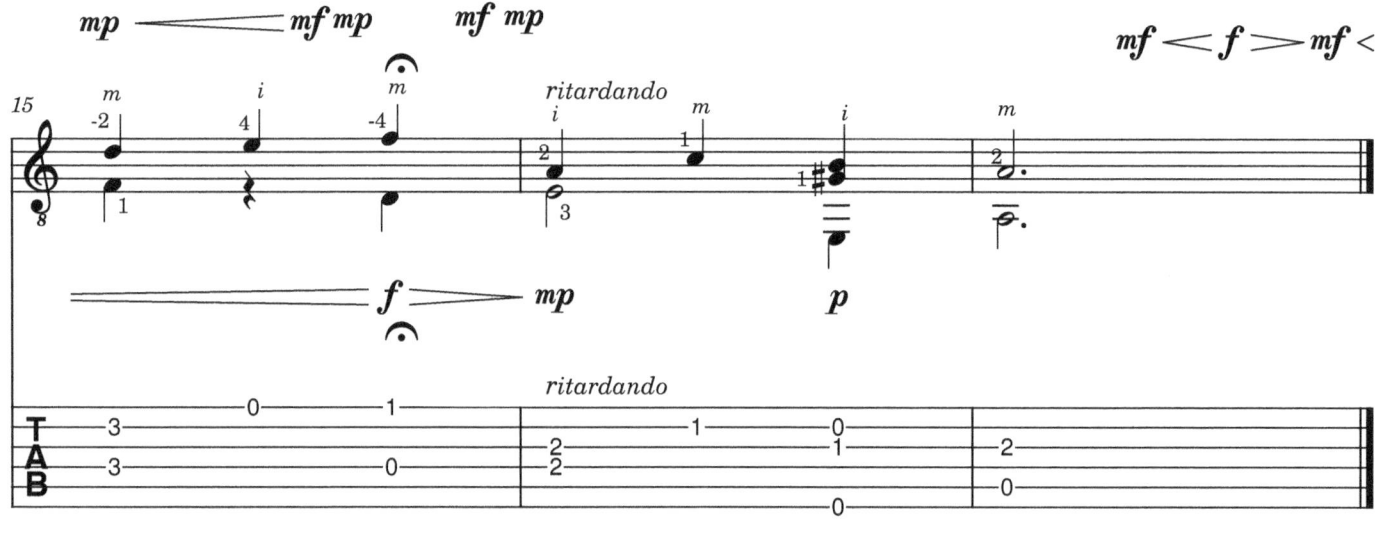

Walz

Dionisio Aguado (1784 - 1849)

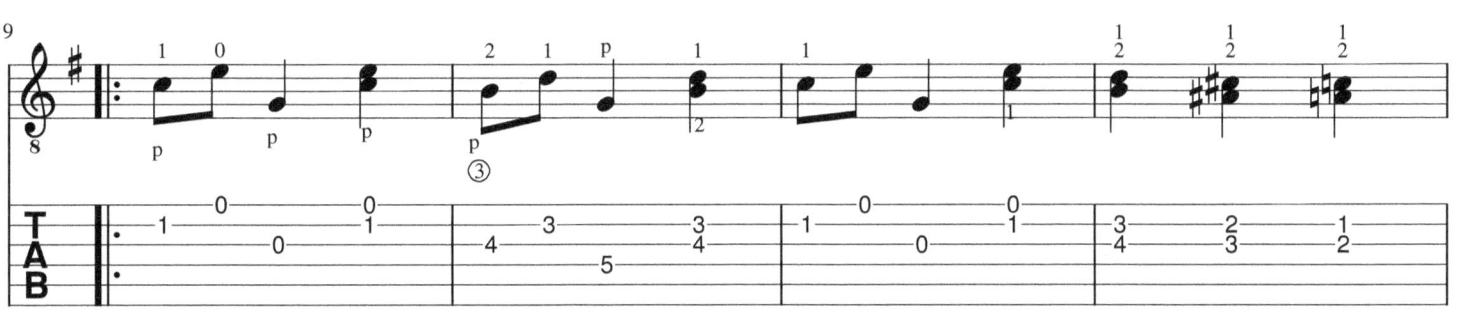

Waltz

Ferdinando Carulli

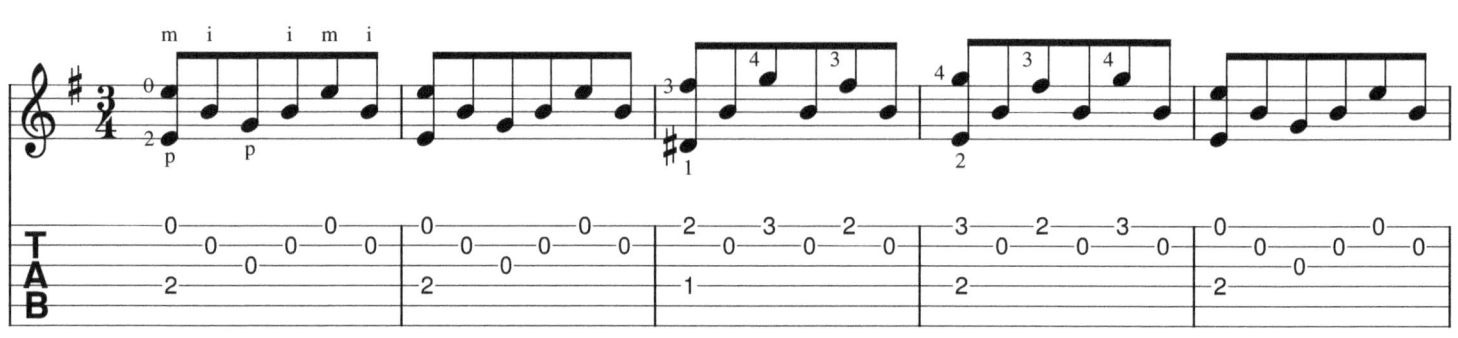

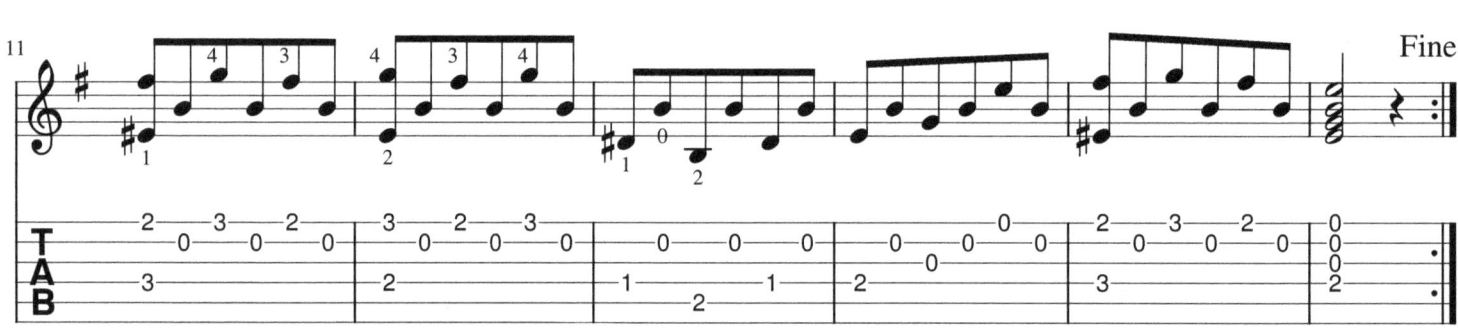
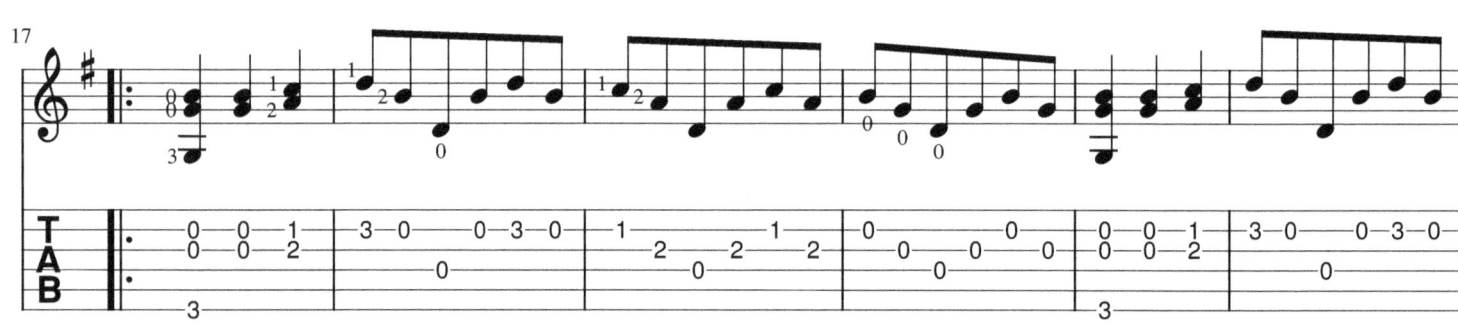

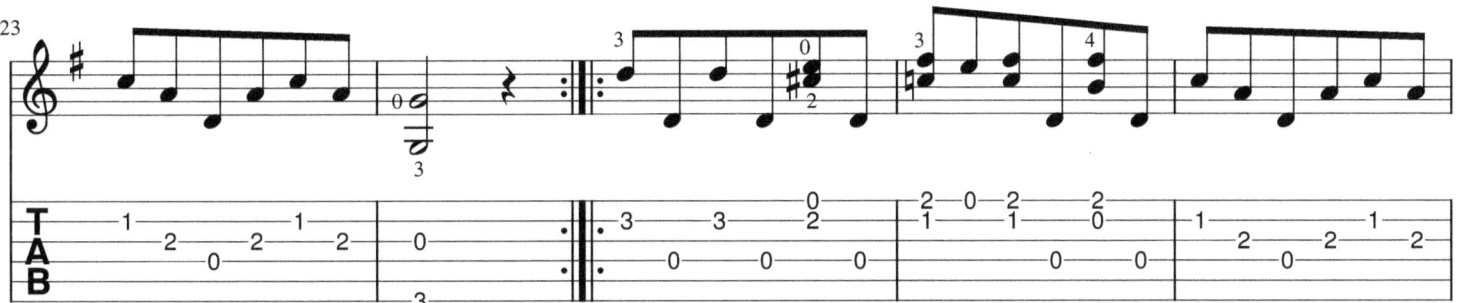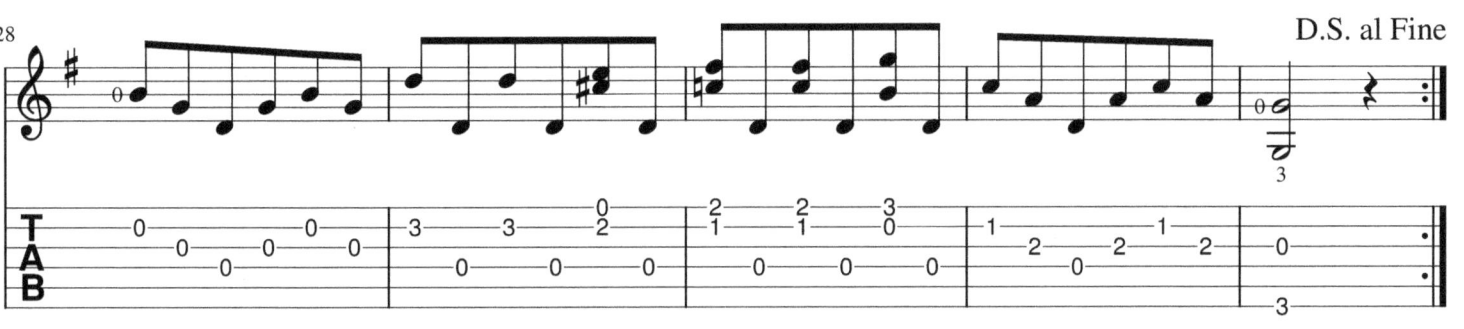

Moderato
op. 39, no. 15

Anton Diabelli (1781-1858)

Andante (2)

Ferdinando Carulli (1770-1841)

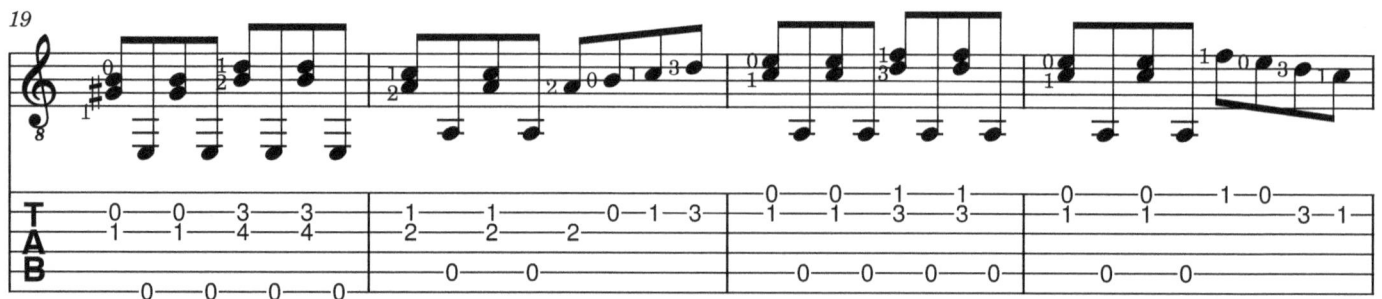
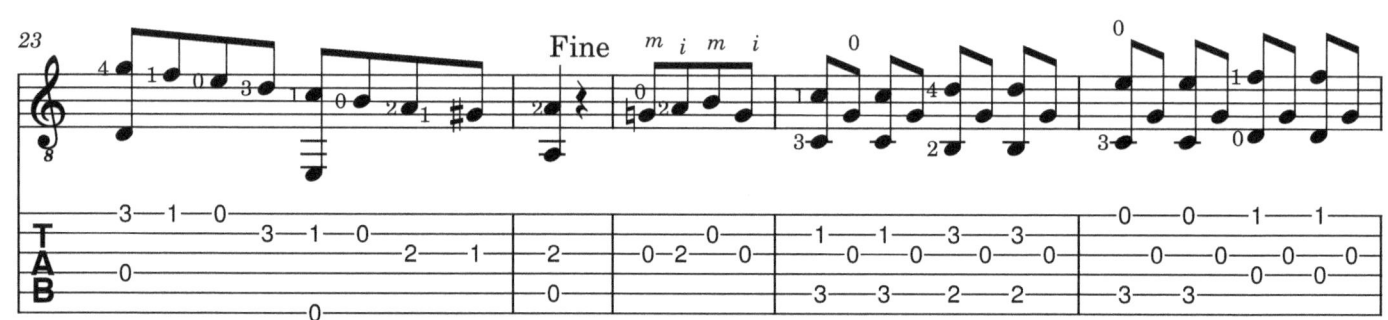
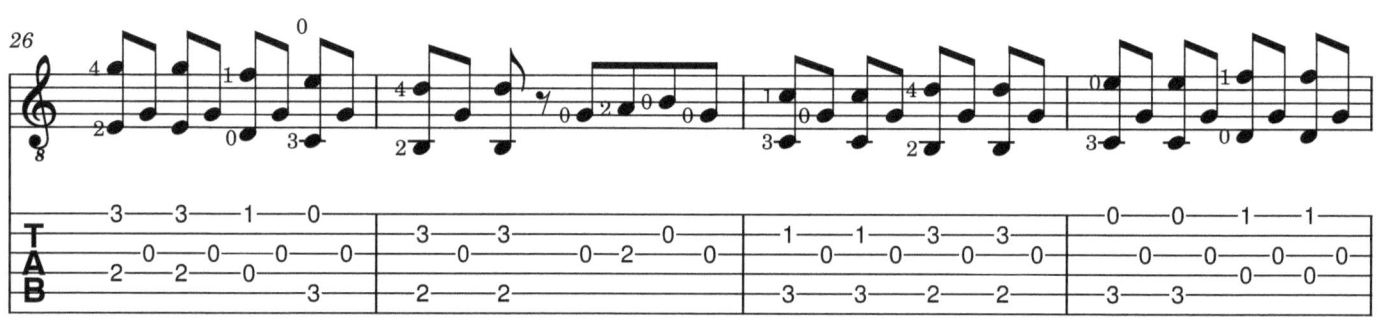
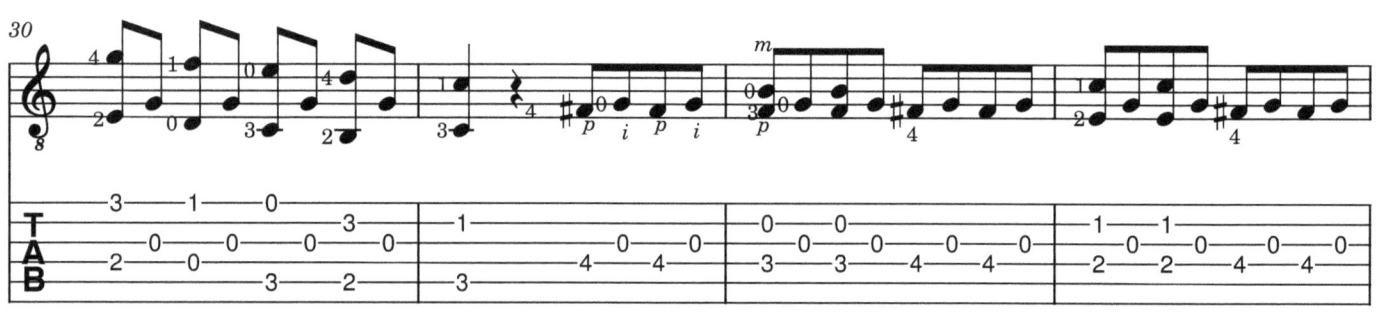
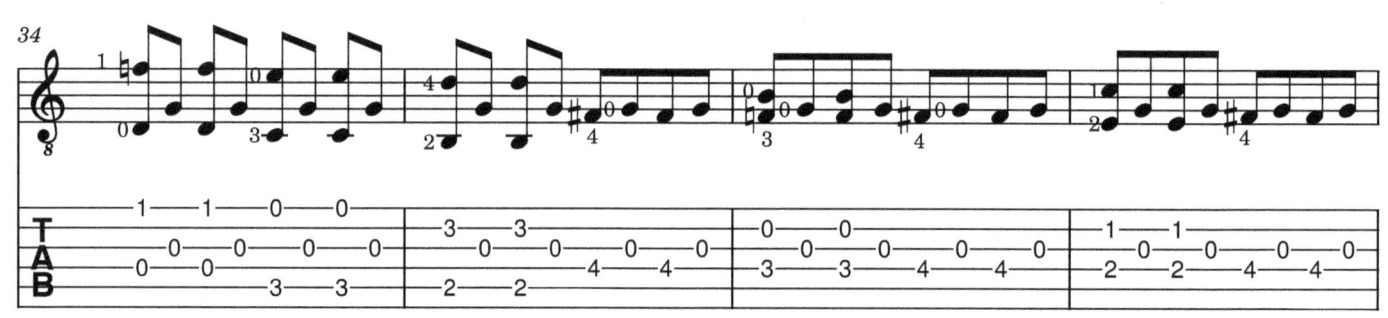

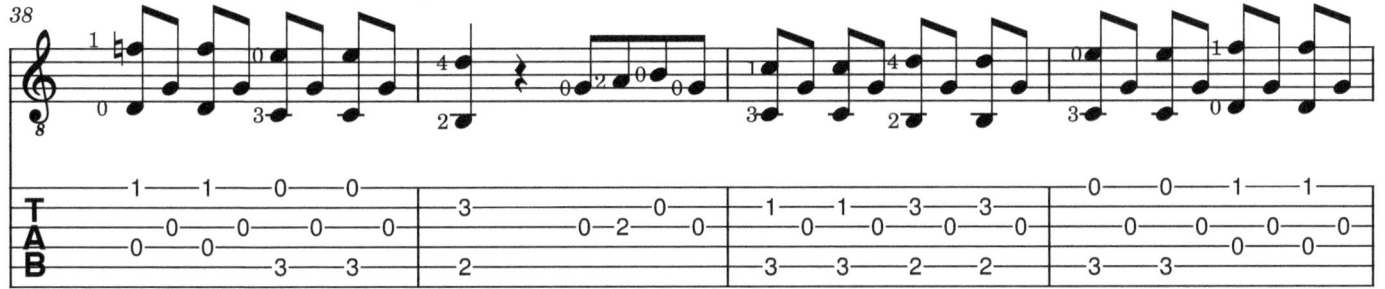

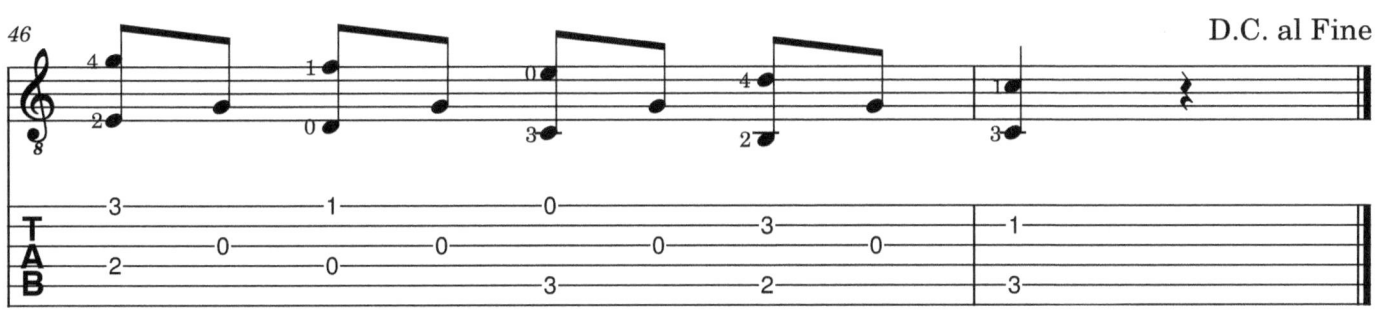

Etude No.9 op.35

Fernando Sor (1778-1839)

Andante.

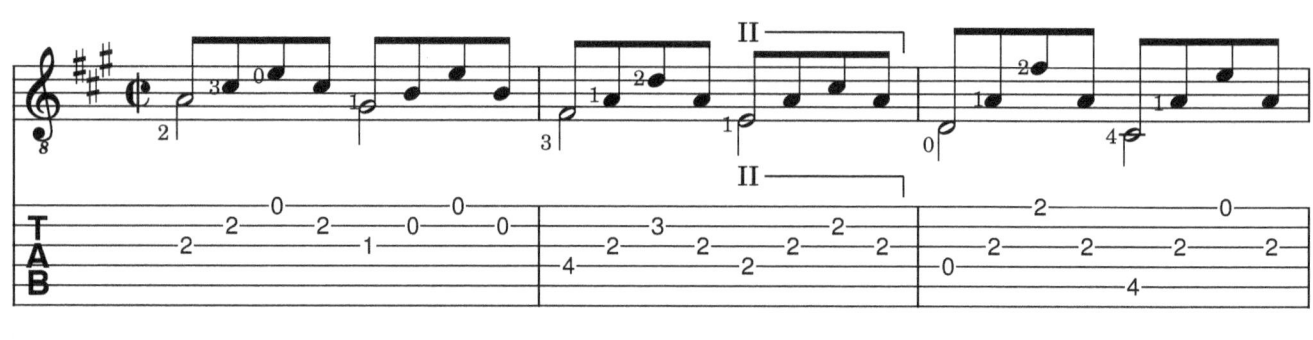
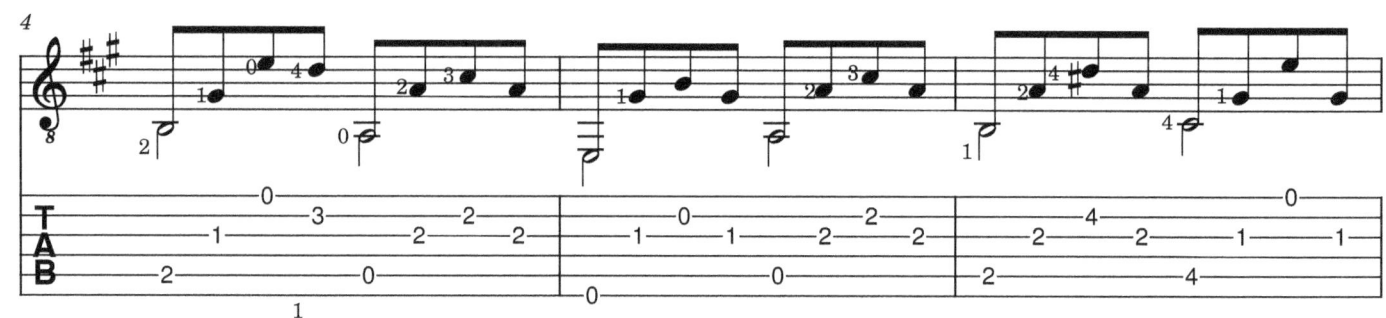
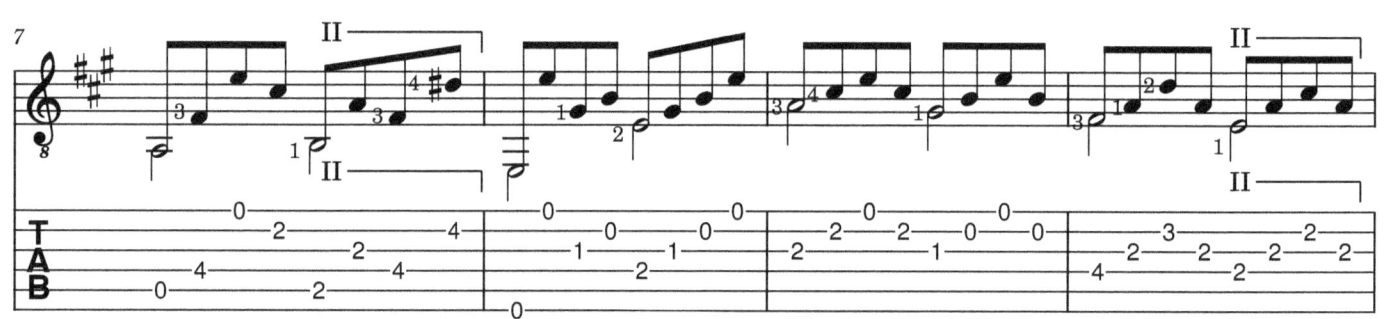
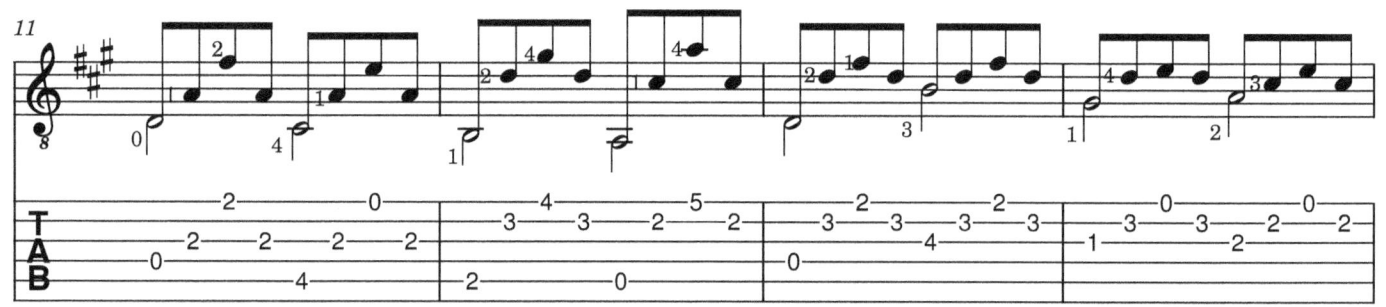
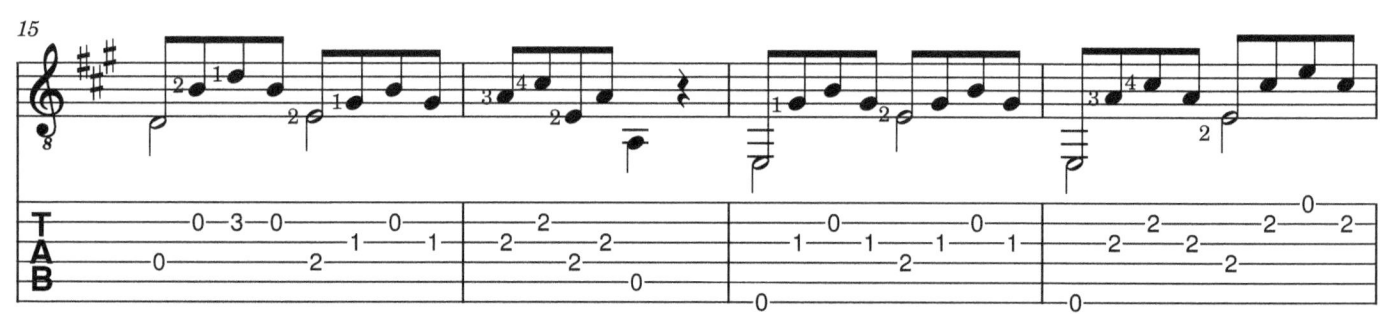

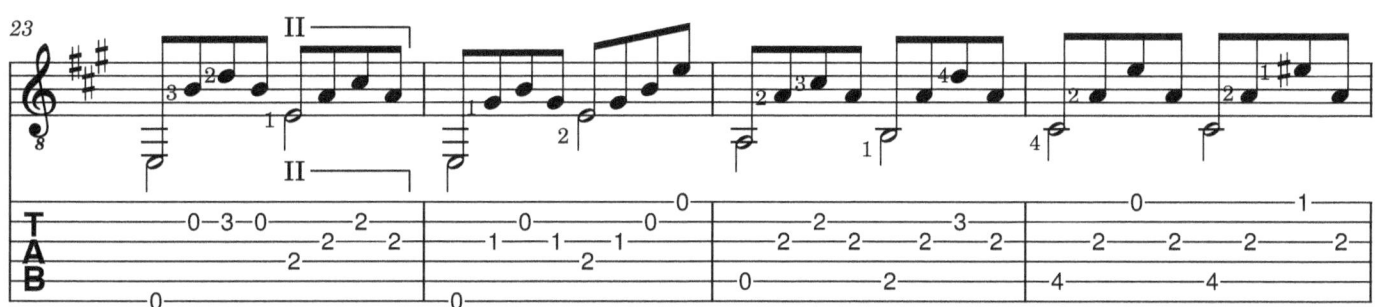
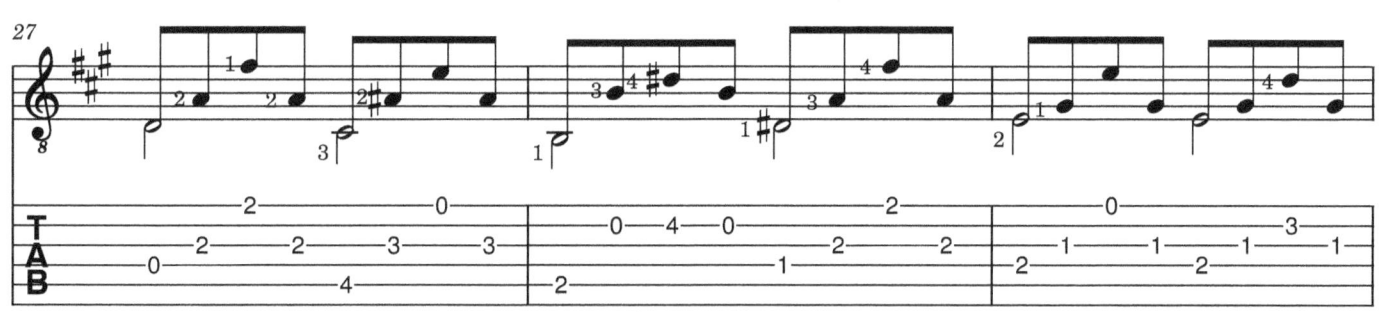

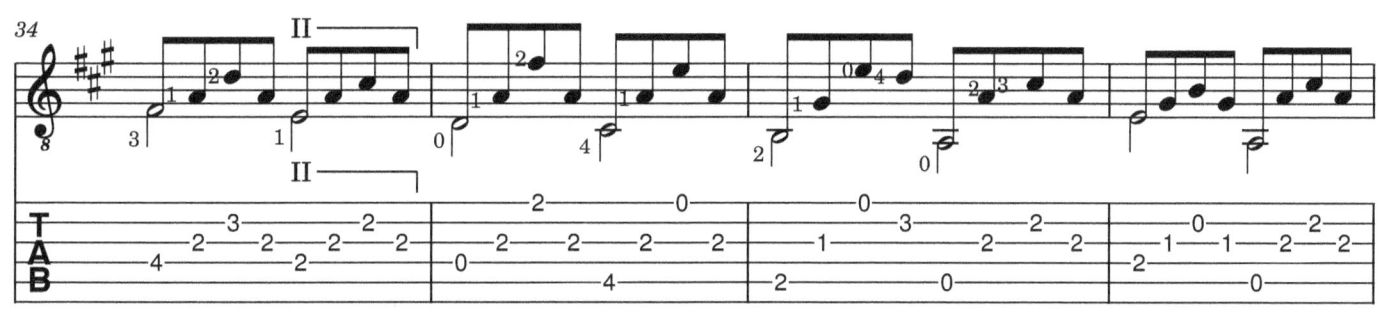

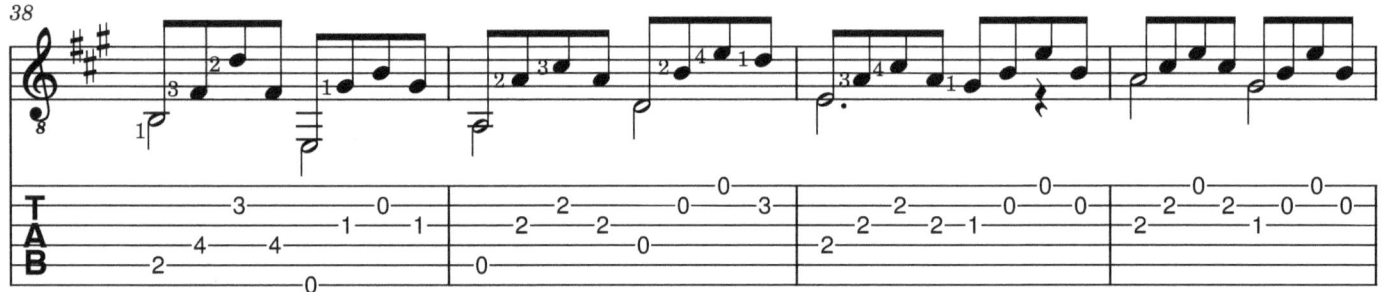
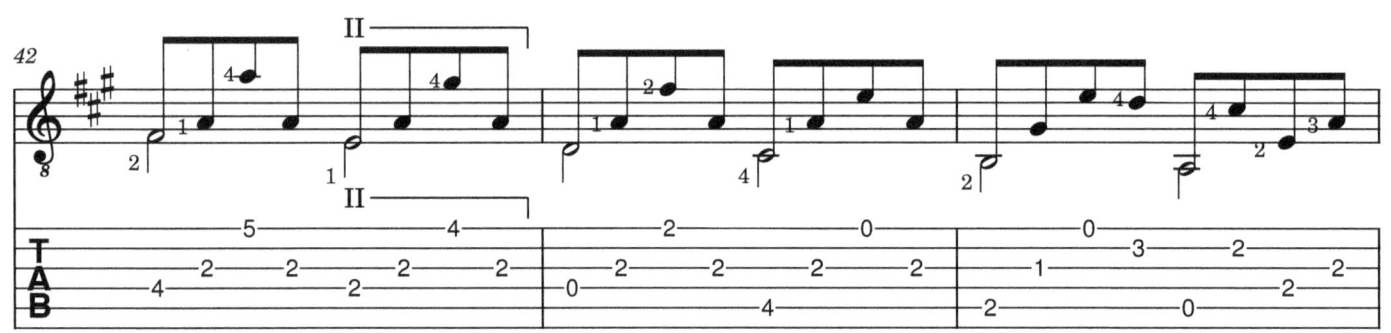
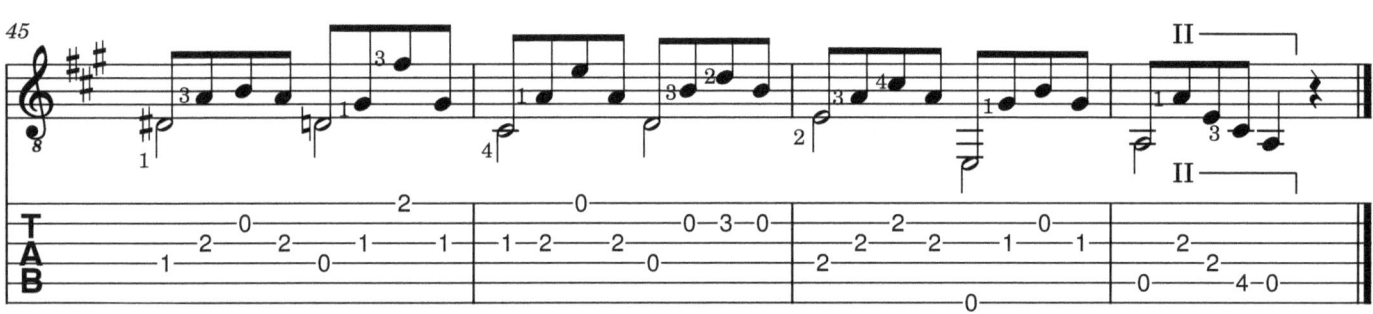

Romantic Era Composers

Matteo Carcassi (1792-1853)

Matteo Carcassi was a famous Italian guitarist and composer. Carcassi began with the piano, but learned guitar when still a child. He quickly gained a reputation as a virtuoso concert guitarist. Carcassi wrote a method for guitar (op. 59) that remains valuable, relevant and interesting, blending technical skills and brilliant romantic music.

Johann Kaspar Mertz (1806-1856)

János Gáspár Mertz was born in Pozsony, Kingdom of Hungary, now Bratislava (Slovakia). A virtuoso, he established a solid reputation as a performer. Mertz's guitar music, followed the pianistic models of Chopin, Mendelssohn, Schubert and Schumann, rather than the classical models of Mozart and Haydn (as did Sor and Aguado), or the bel canto style of Rossini (as did Giuliani).

Napoleon Coste (1805 – 1883)

Napoleon is french and is a major figure in guitar composition of the mid-nineteenth century. Napoleon was taught by his mother at a very early age. Napoleon later became Fernando Sor's student and quickly established himself as the leading French virtuoso guitarist. Napoleon is the first composer to transcribe guitar music of the 17th century to the modern era.

Francisco Tarrega (1852-1909)

Tárrega is considered to have laid the foundations for 20th century classical guitar and for increasing interest in the guitar as a recital instrument. Tárrega preferred small intimate performances over the concert stage. Some believe this was because he played without the nails needed for volume. Others say this was related to his childhood trauma.

This page left blank intentionally.

(to avoid awkward page turns)

Allegretto

Matteo Carcassi (1796-1853)

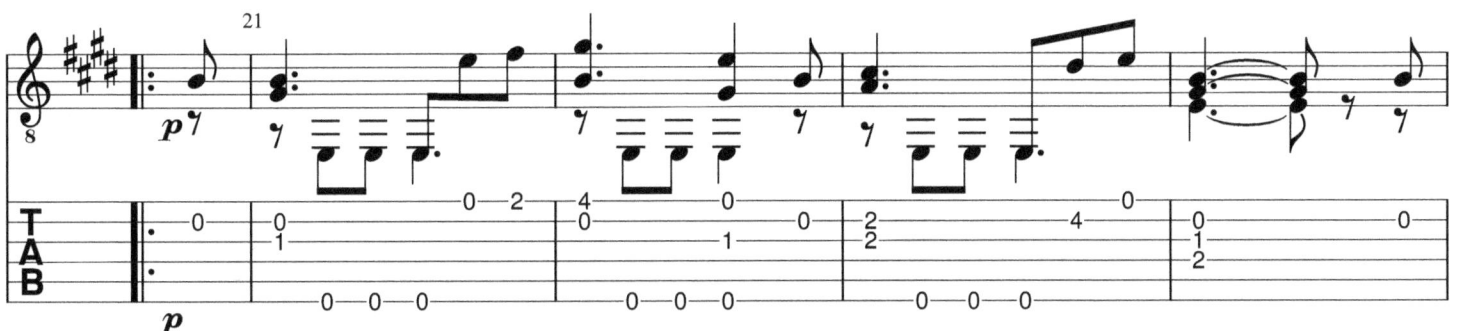

Allegretto

Matteo Carcassi (1796-1853)

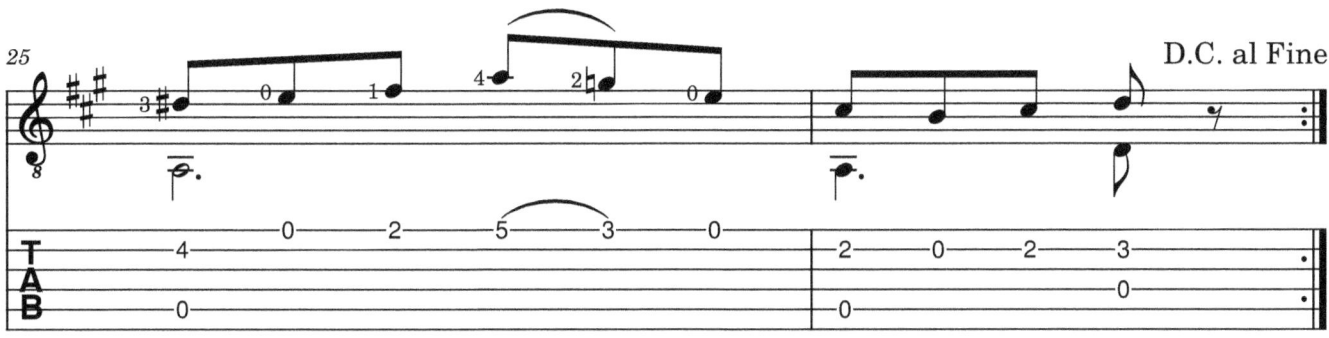

ANDANTINO

Mateo Carcassi (1796-1853)

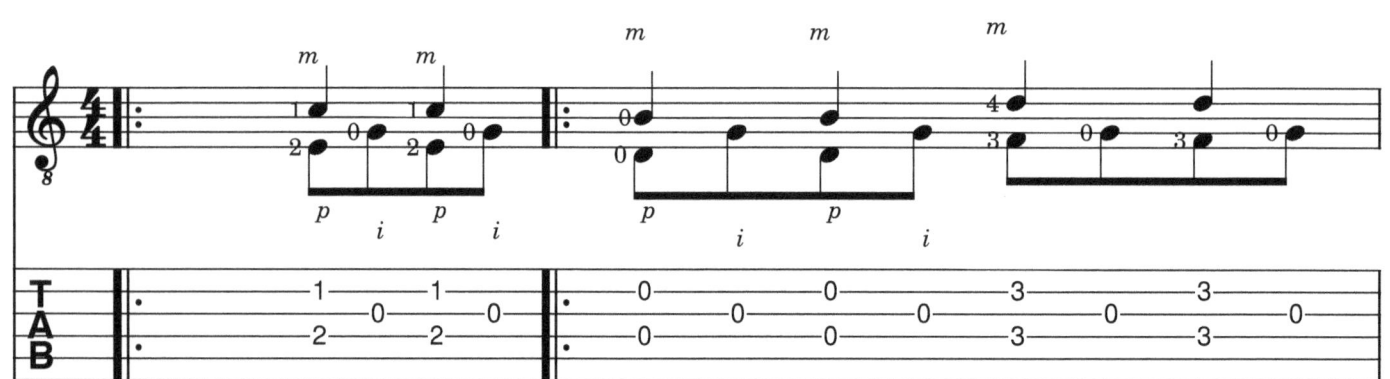
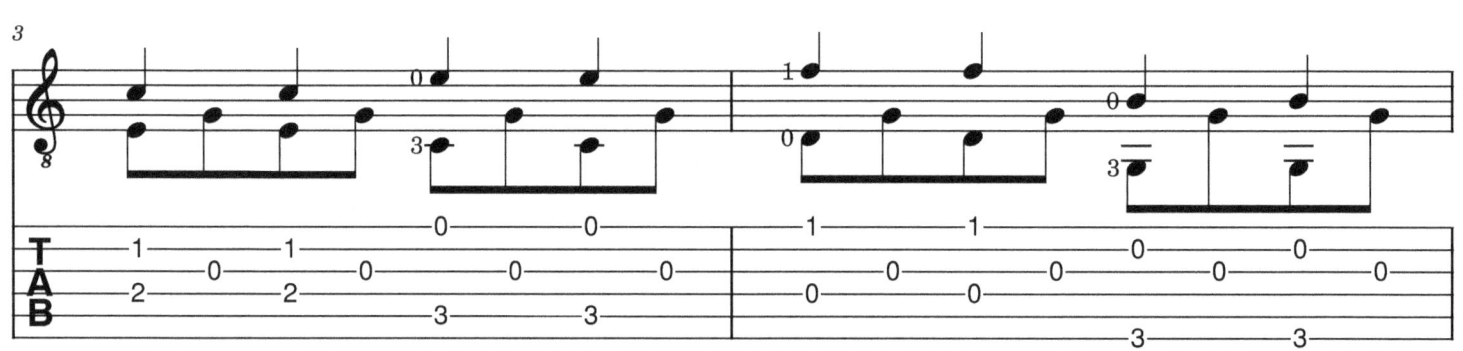
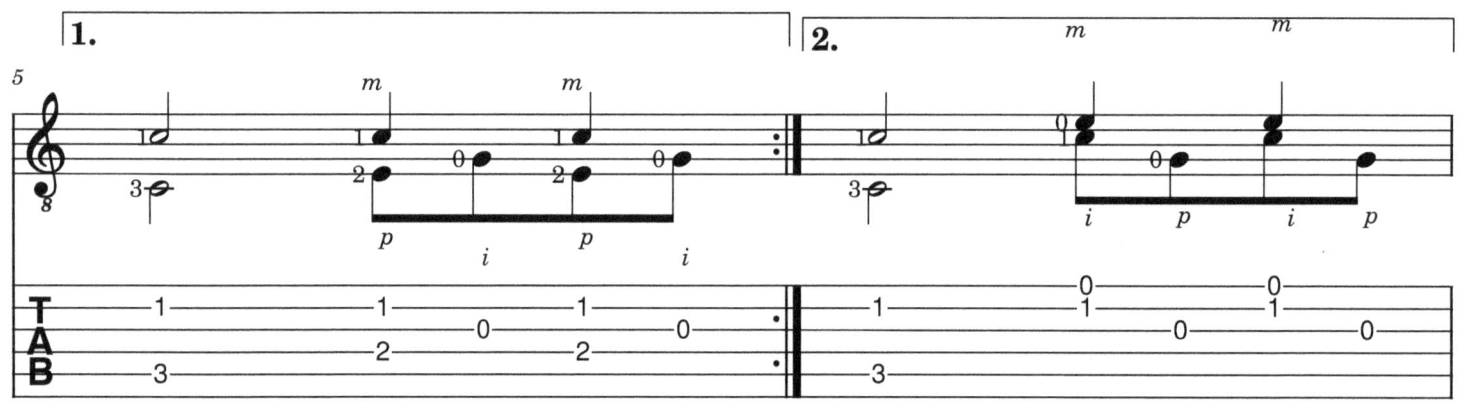
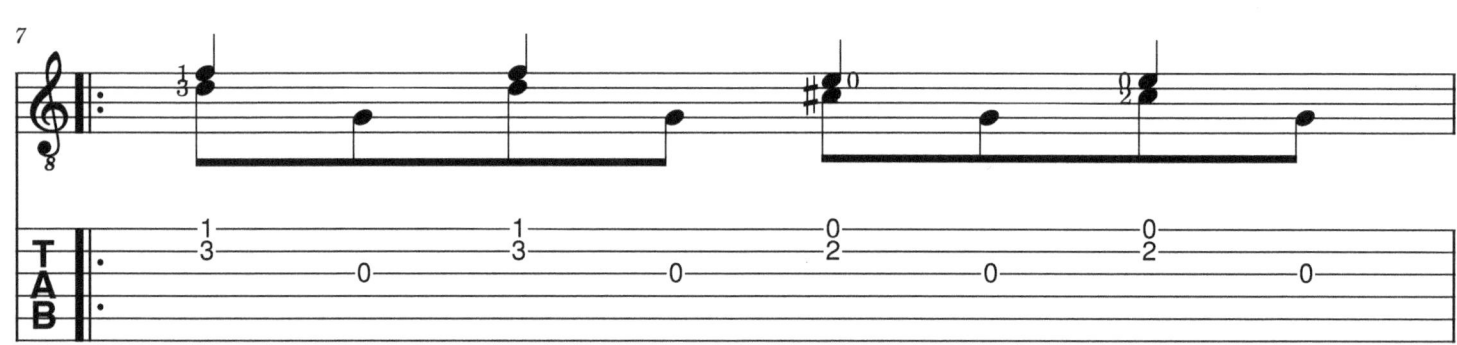

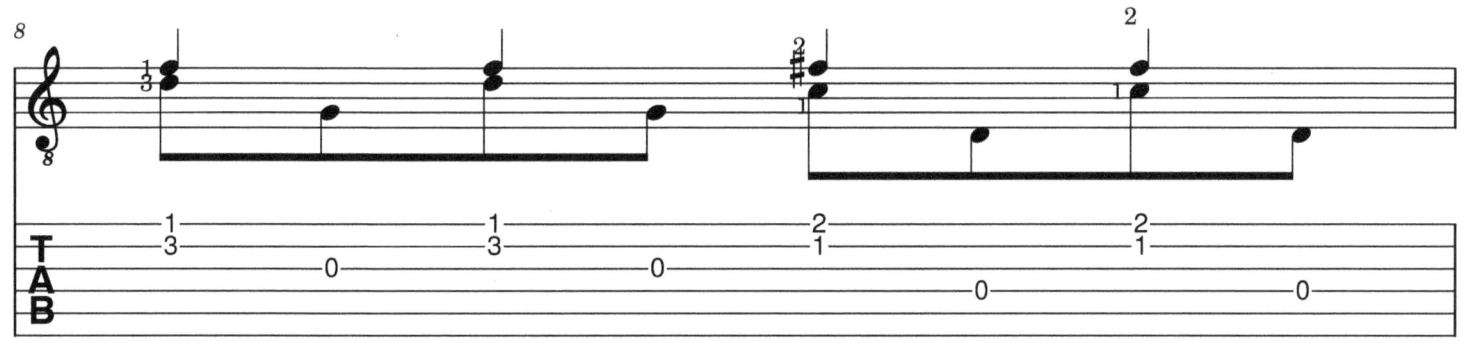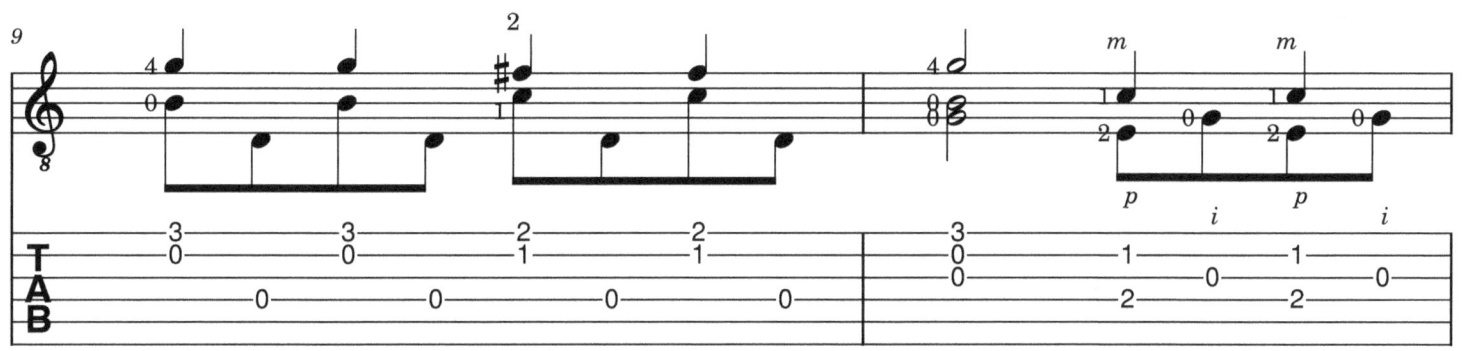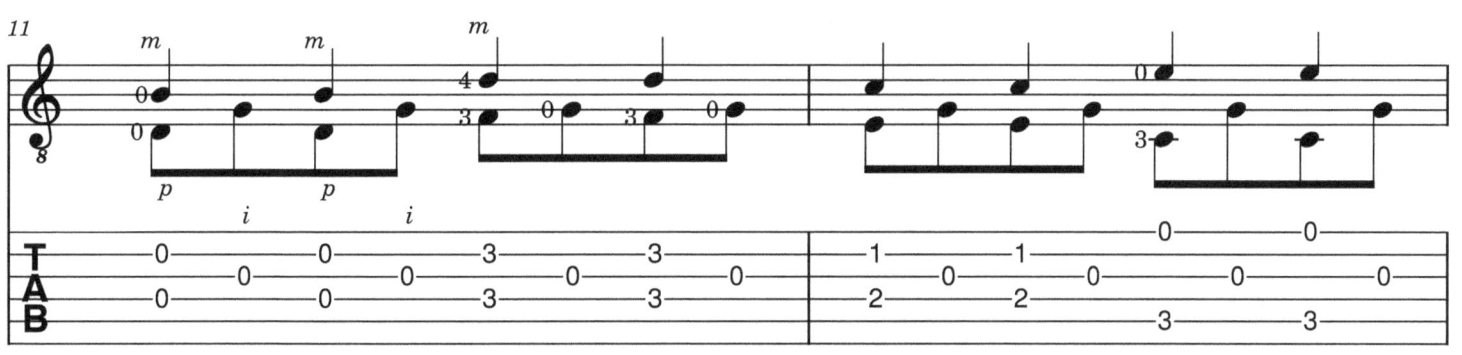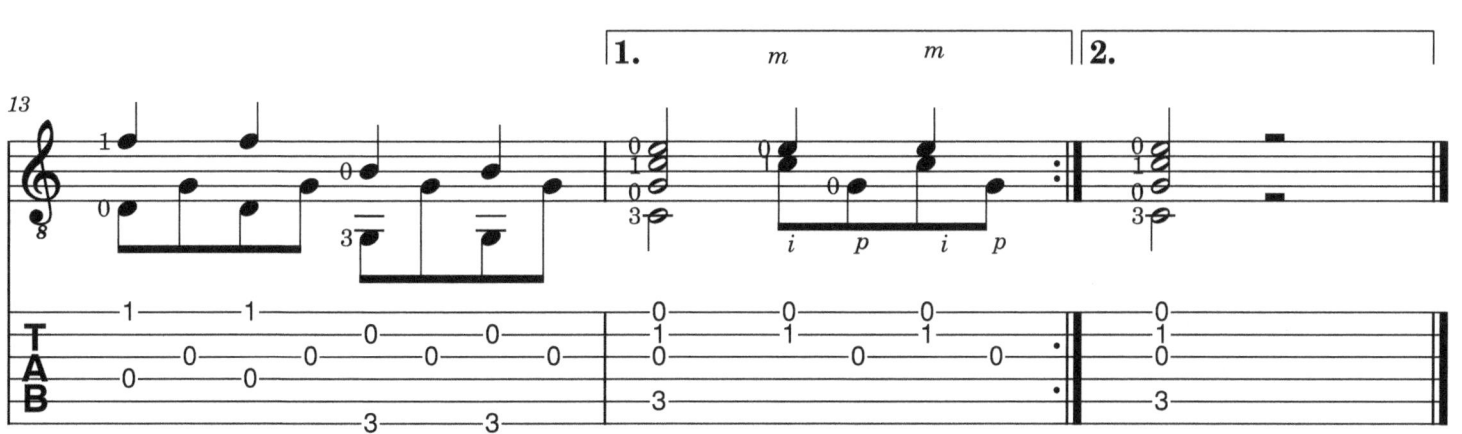

Study in A Minor

Napoleon Coste (1805-1883)

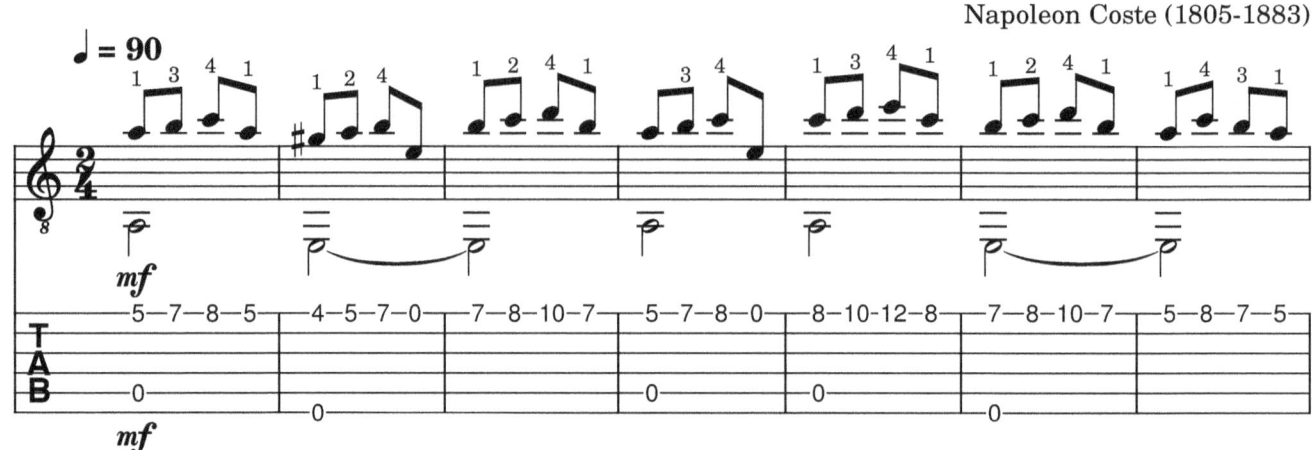
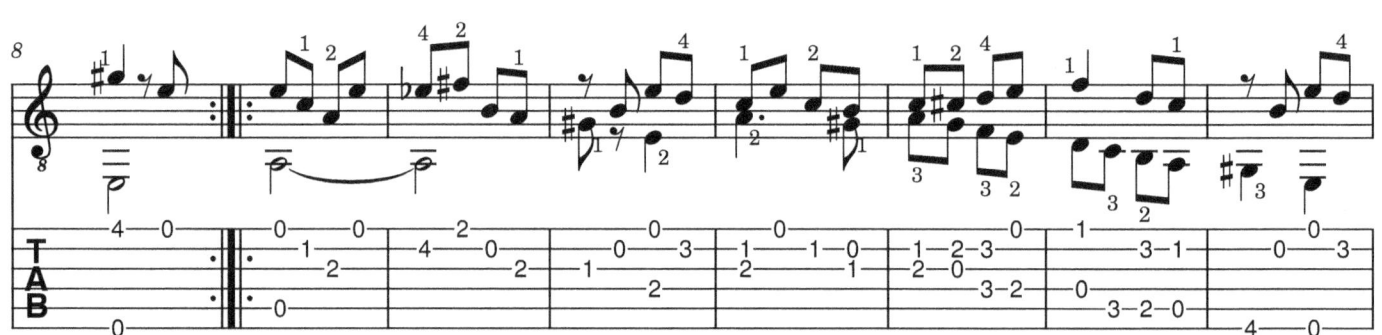
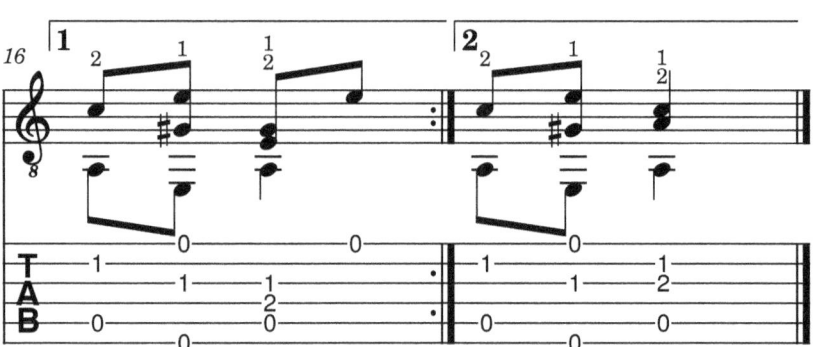

Etude

Francisco Tarrega (1852-1909)

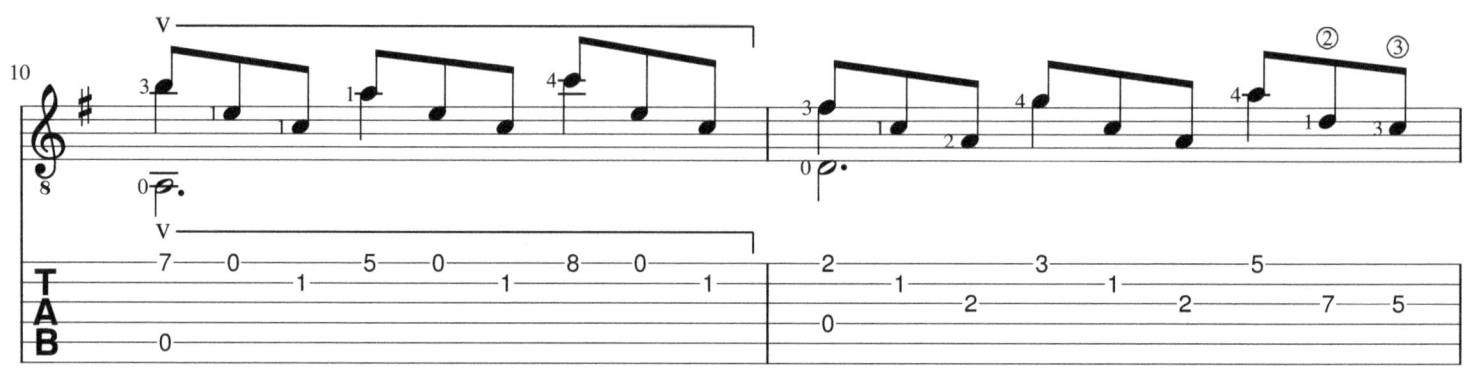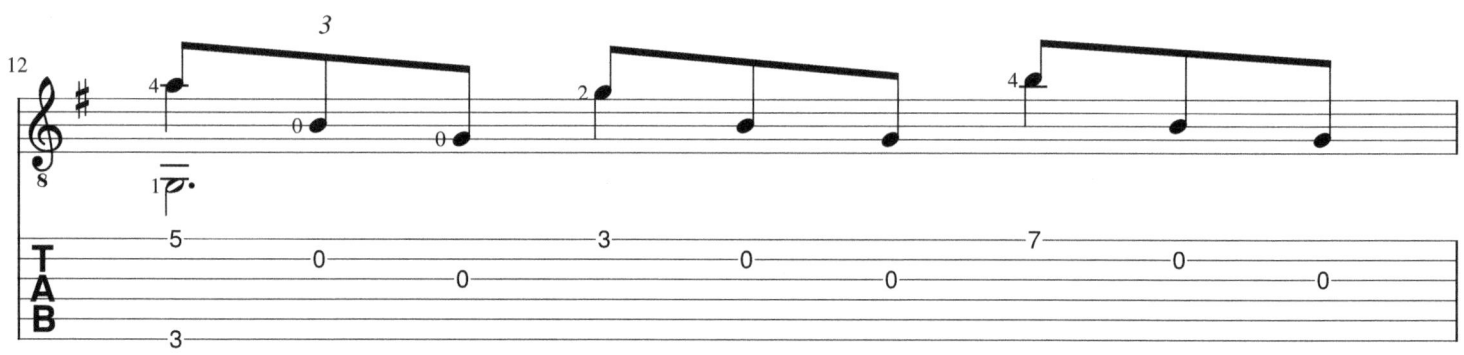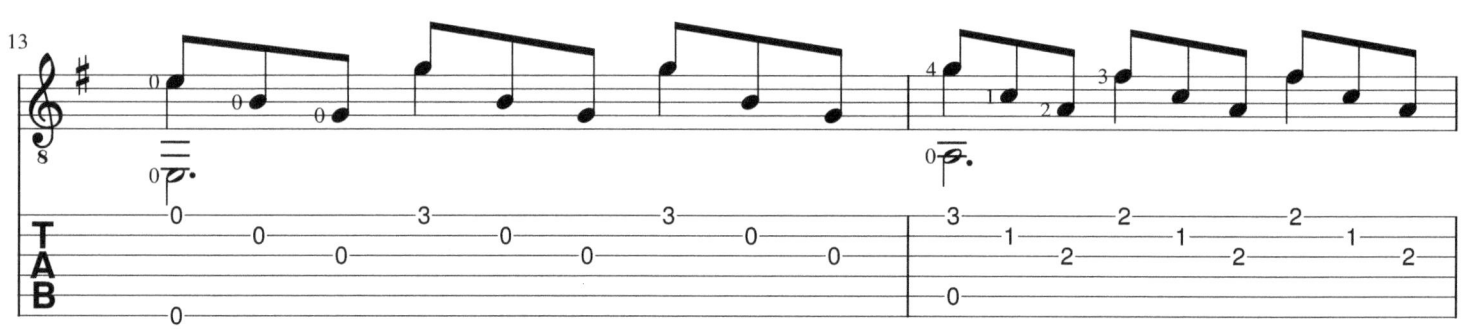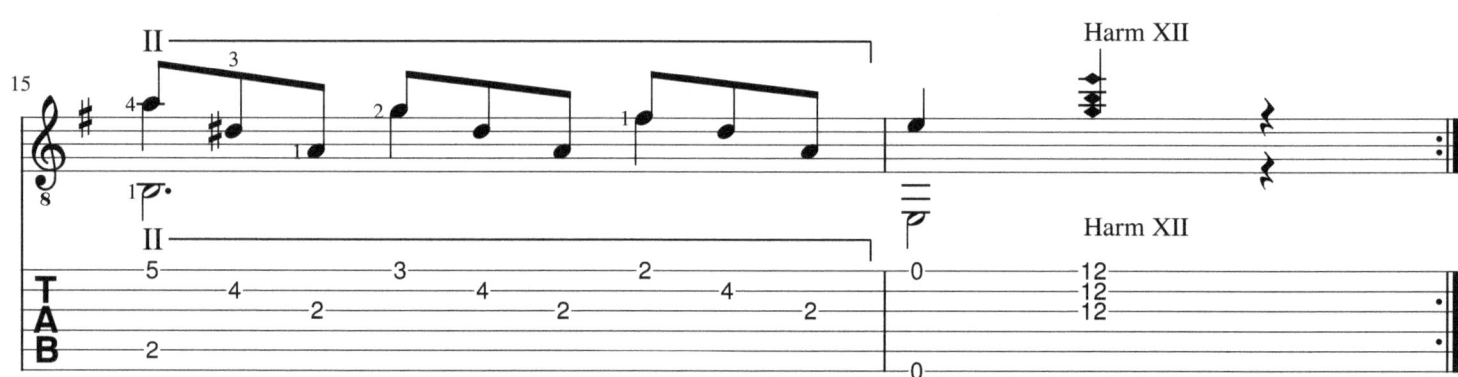

Etude in G

Johann Kaspar Mertz (1806 - 1856)

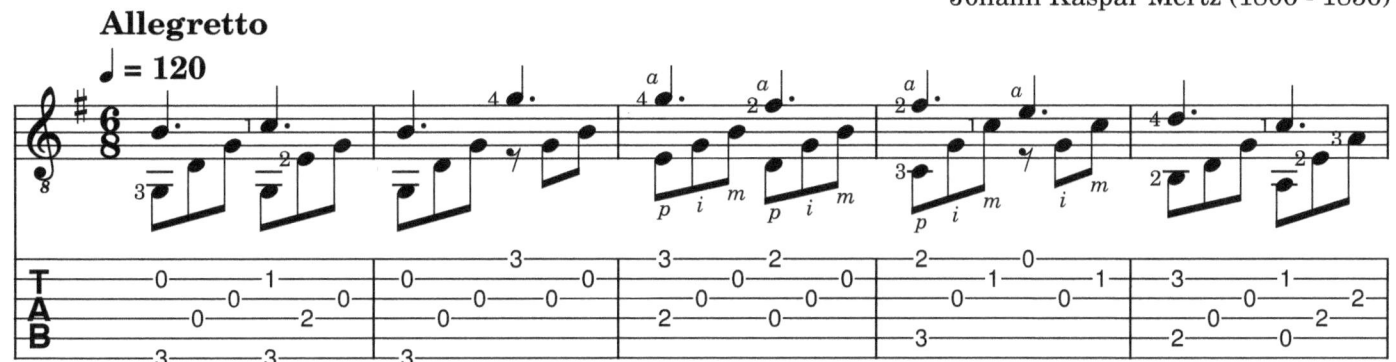
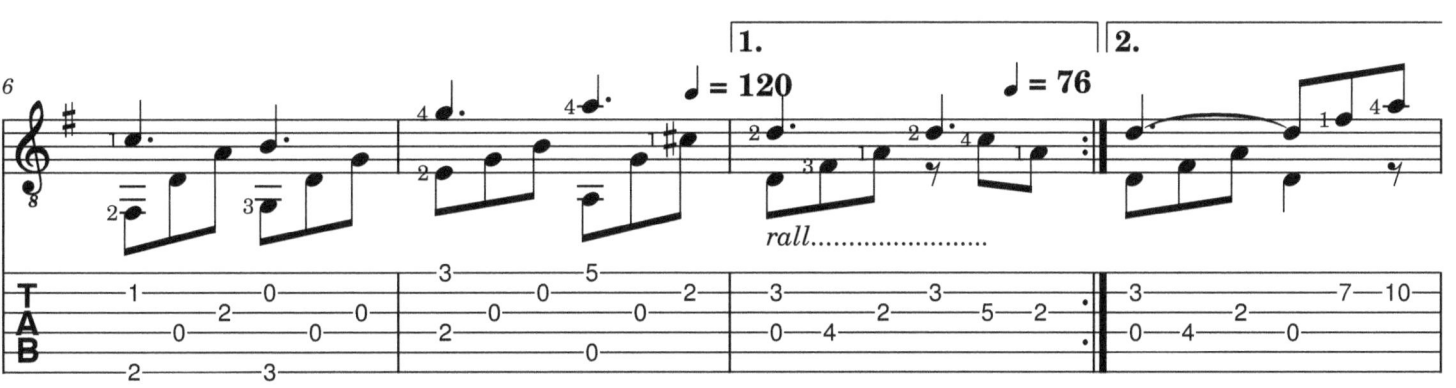
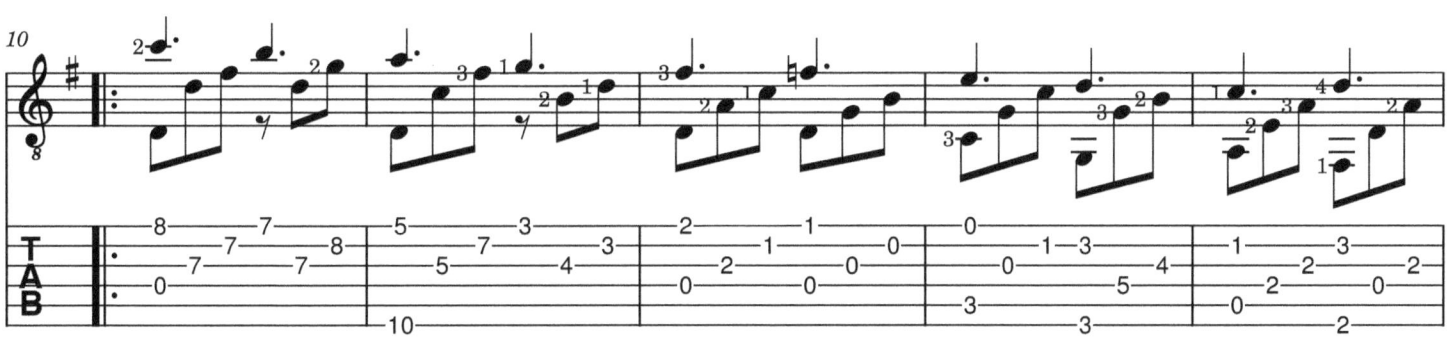
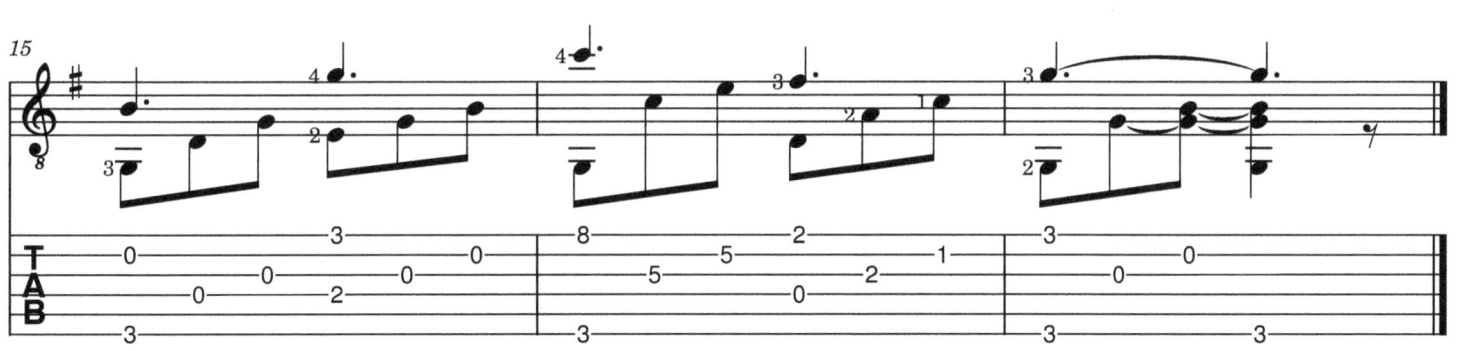

Ländler

Johann Kaspar Mertz (1806 - 1856)

Allegretto.

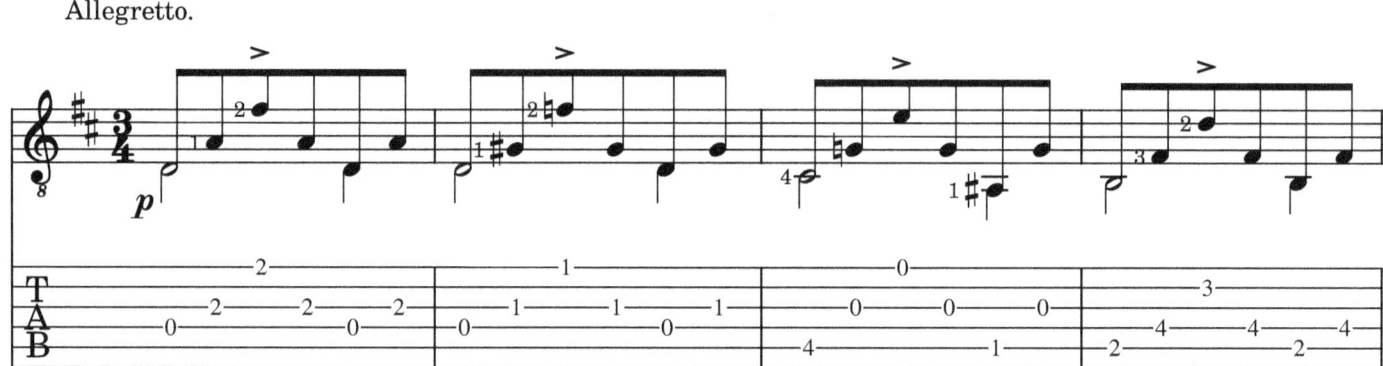
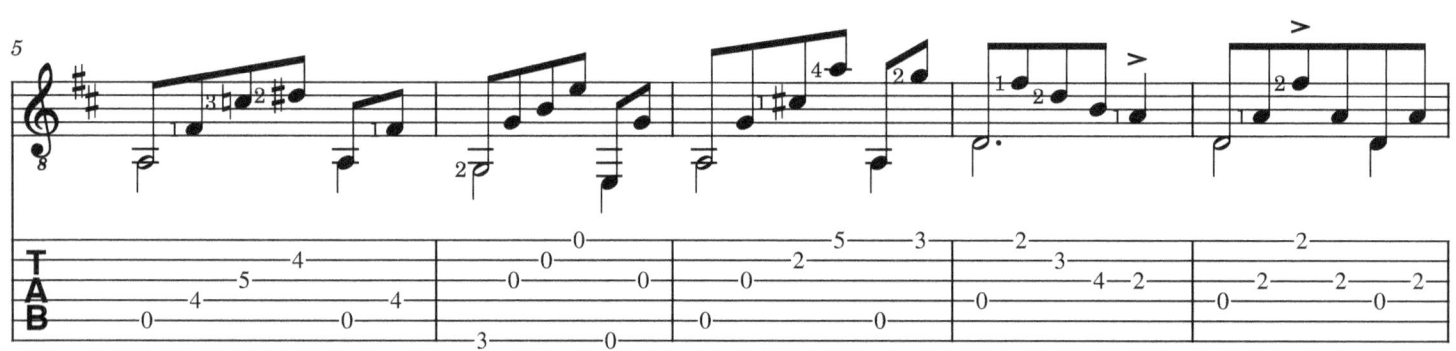
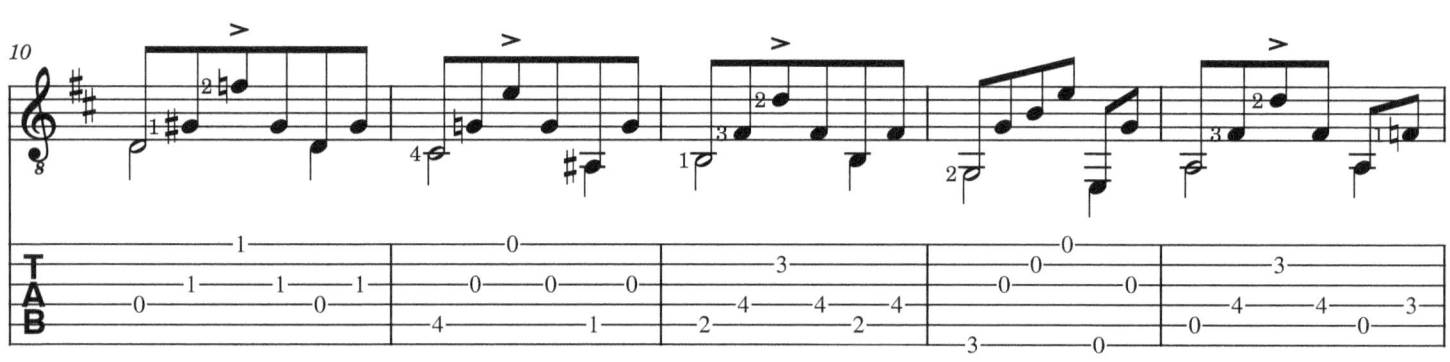
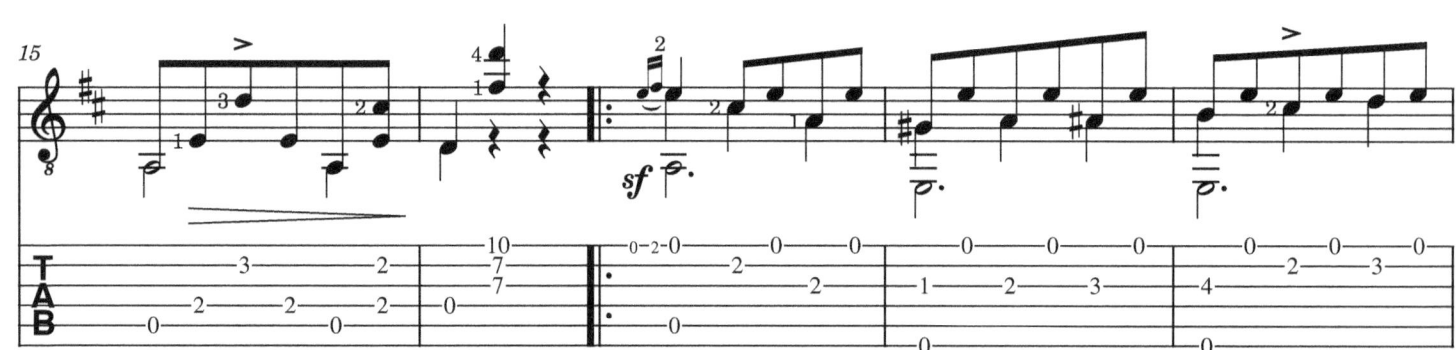

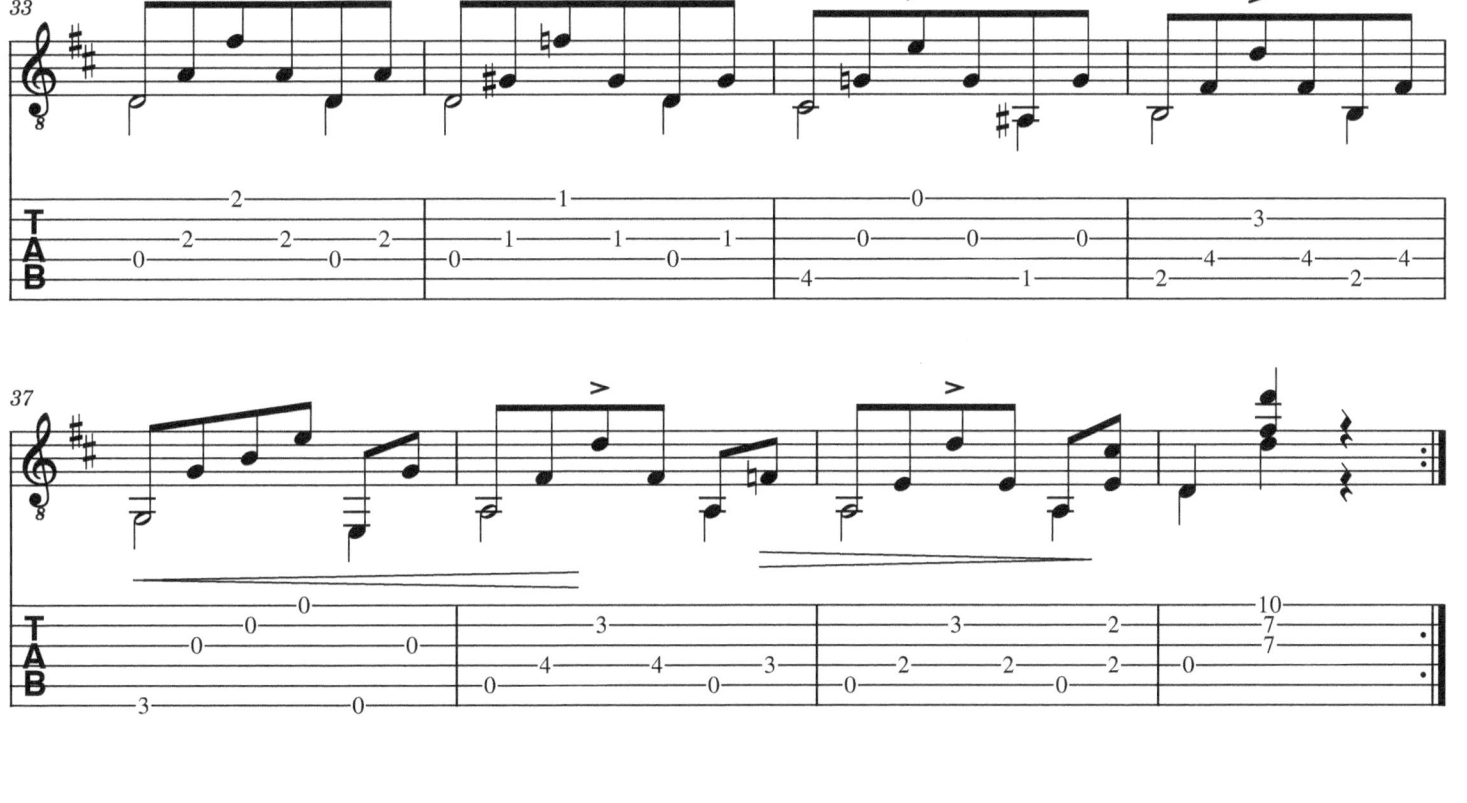

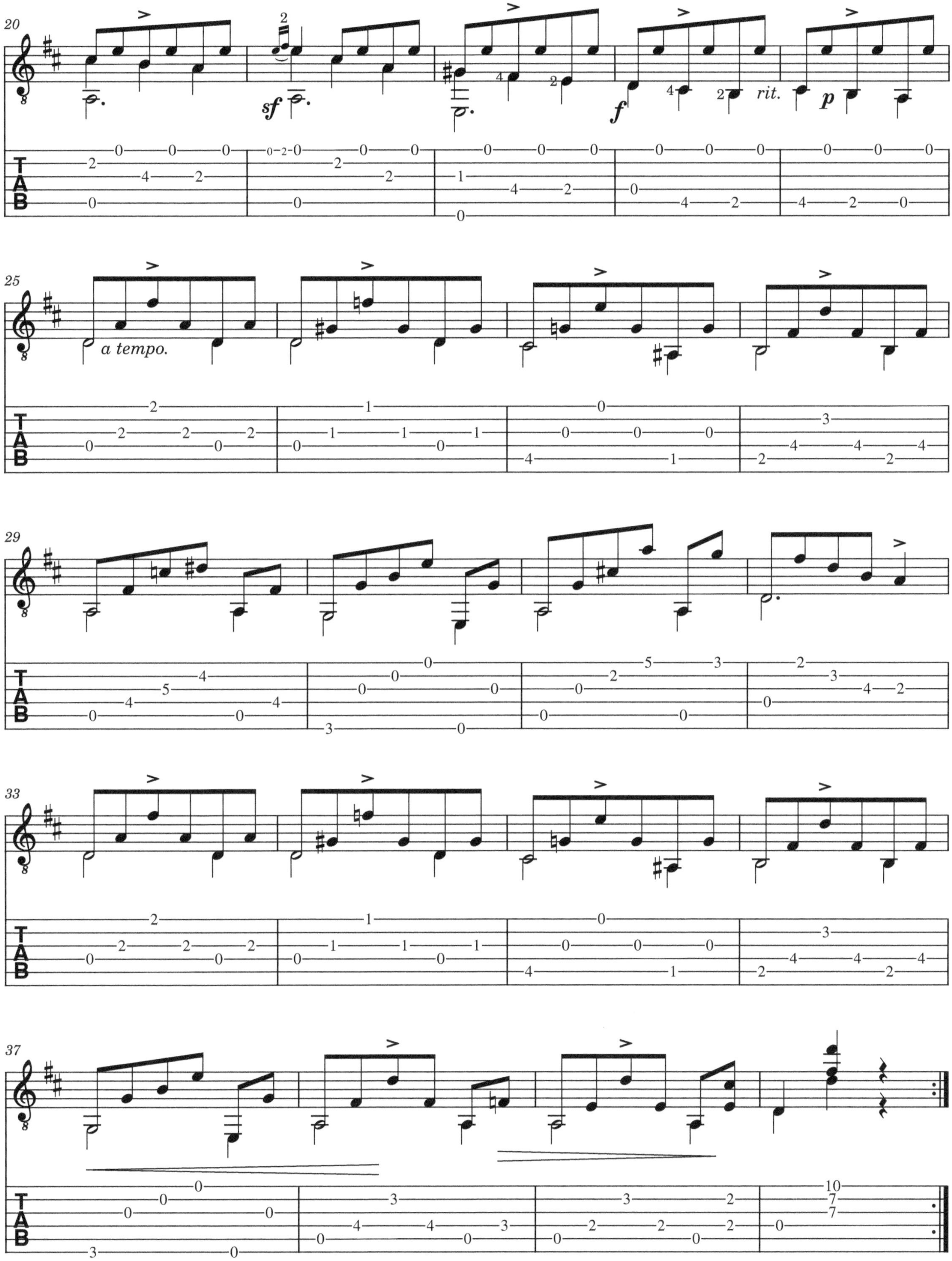
20
sf
f
rit.
p
25
a tempo.
29
33
37

Lagrima

Francisco Tarrega (1852-1909)

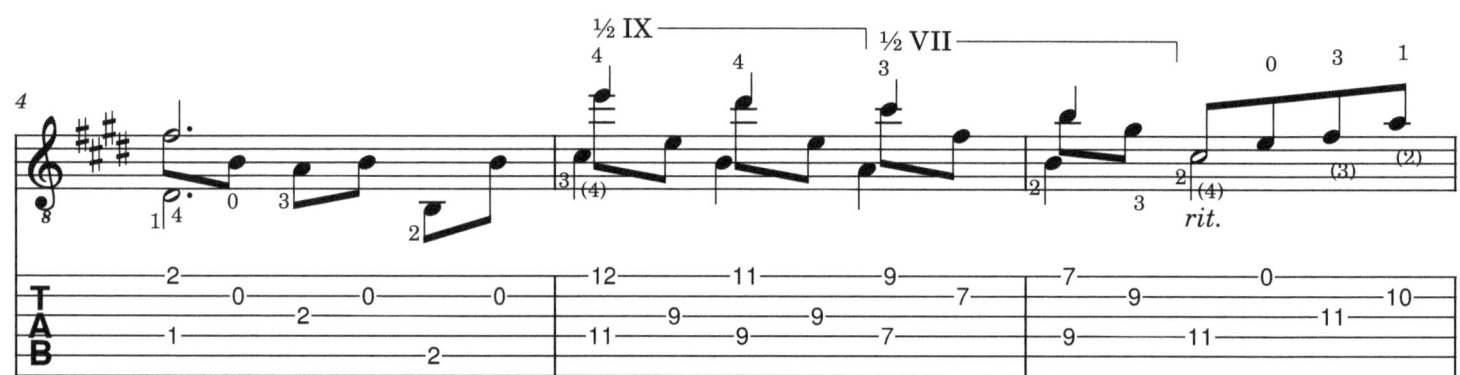
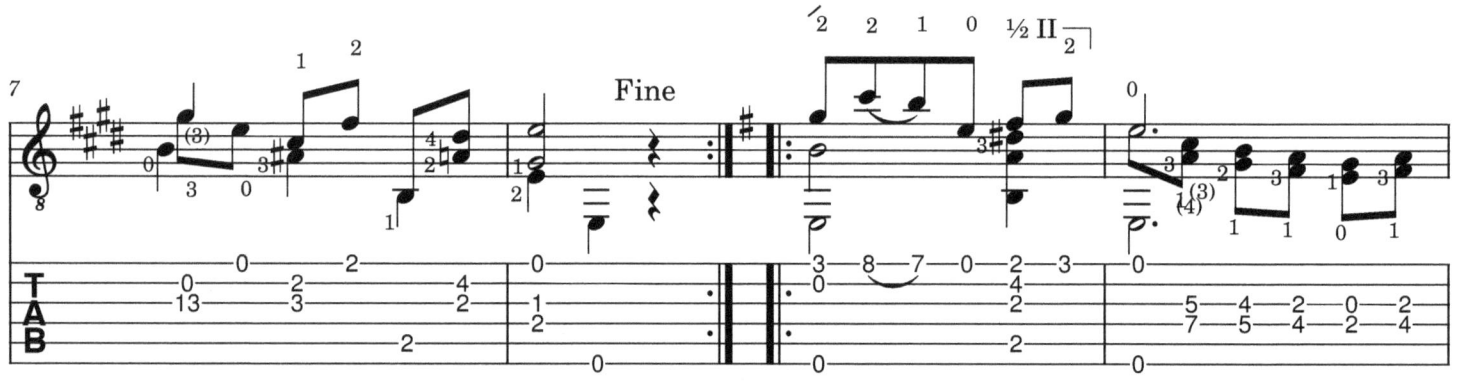

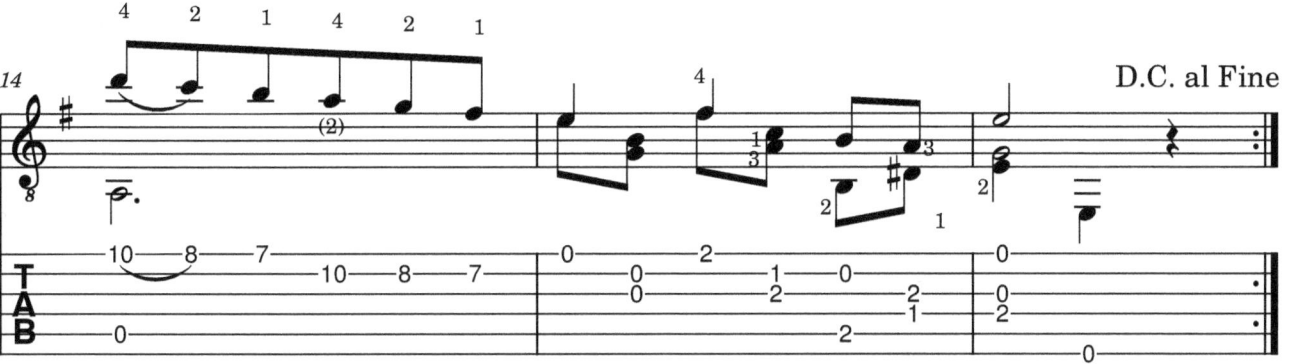

Pastoral

Matteo Carcassi (1796-1853)

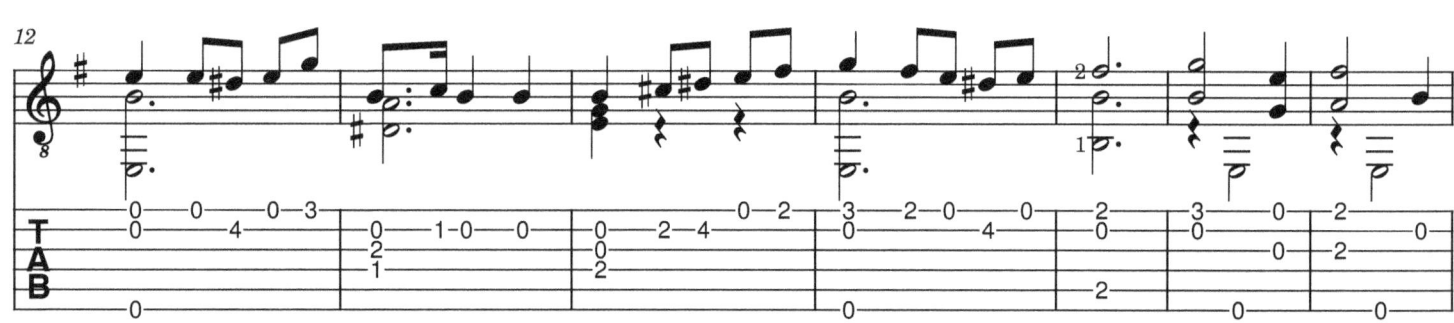

Romance

Johann Kaspar Mertz (1806 - 1856)

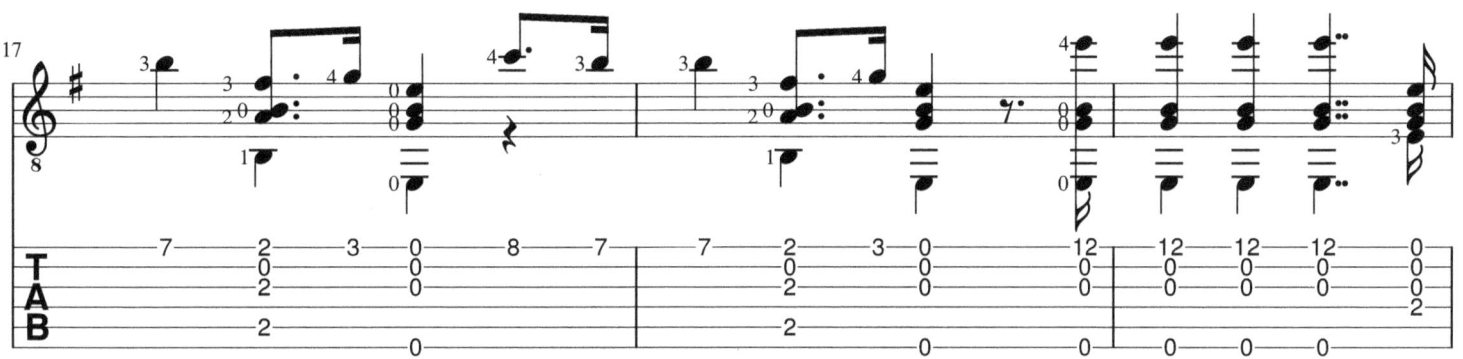
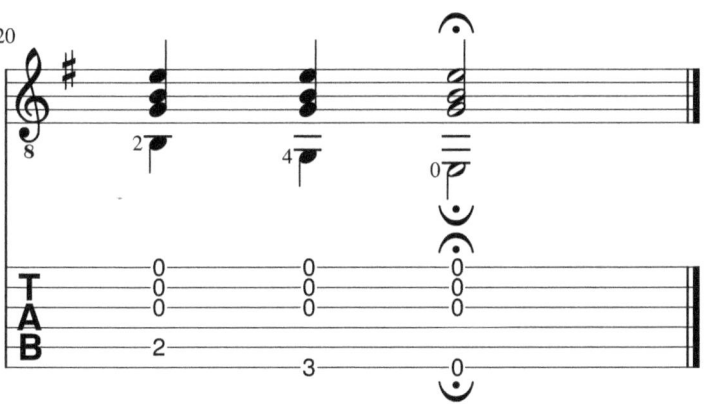

Study in A minor

Matteo Carcassi (1796 - 1853)

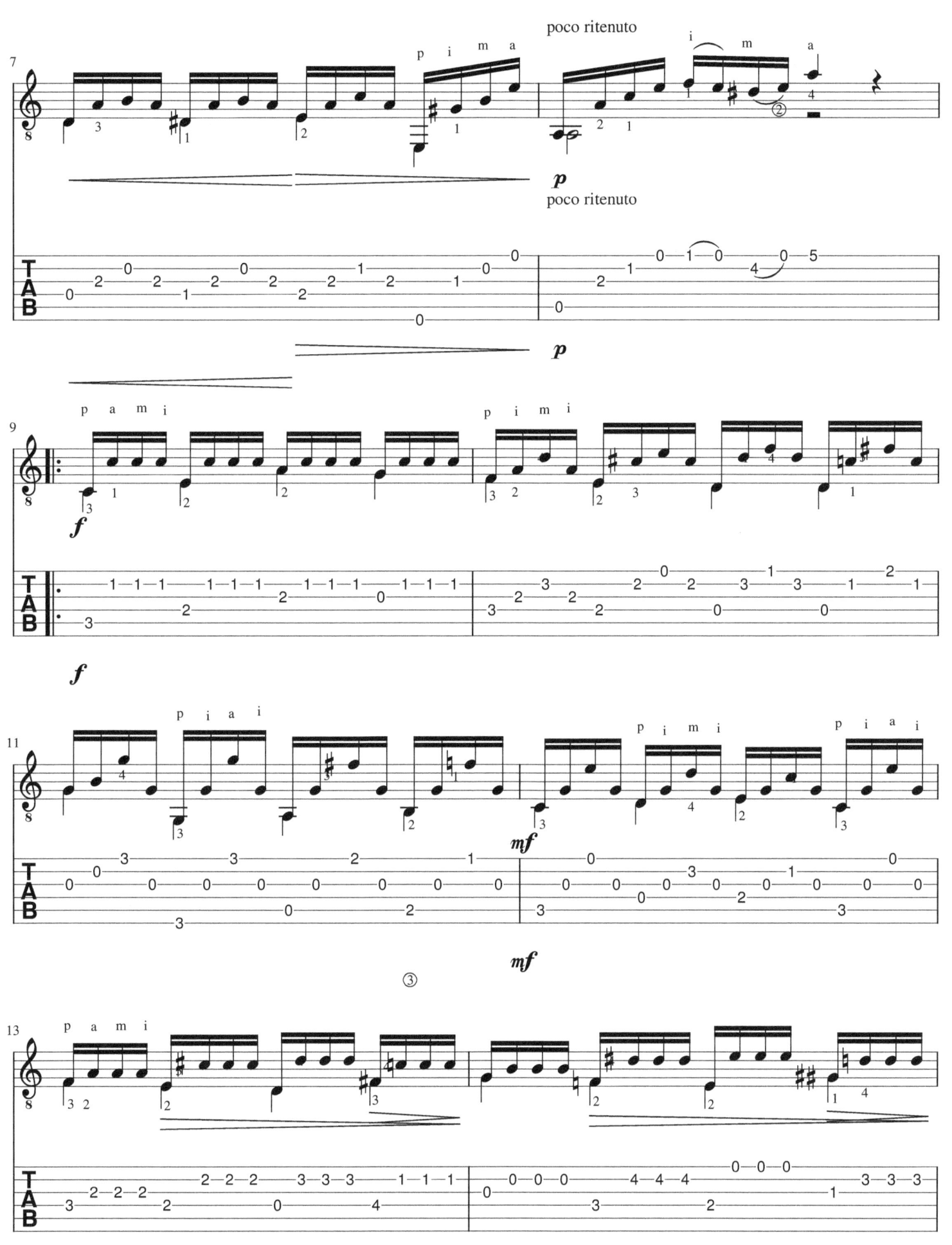

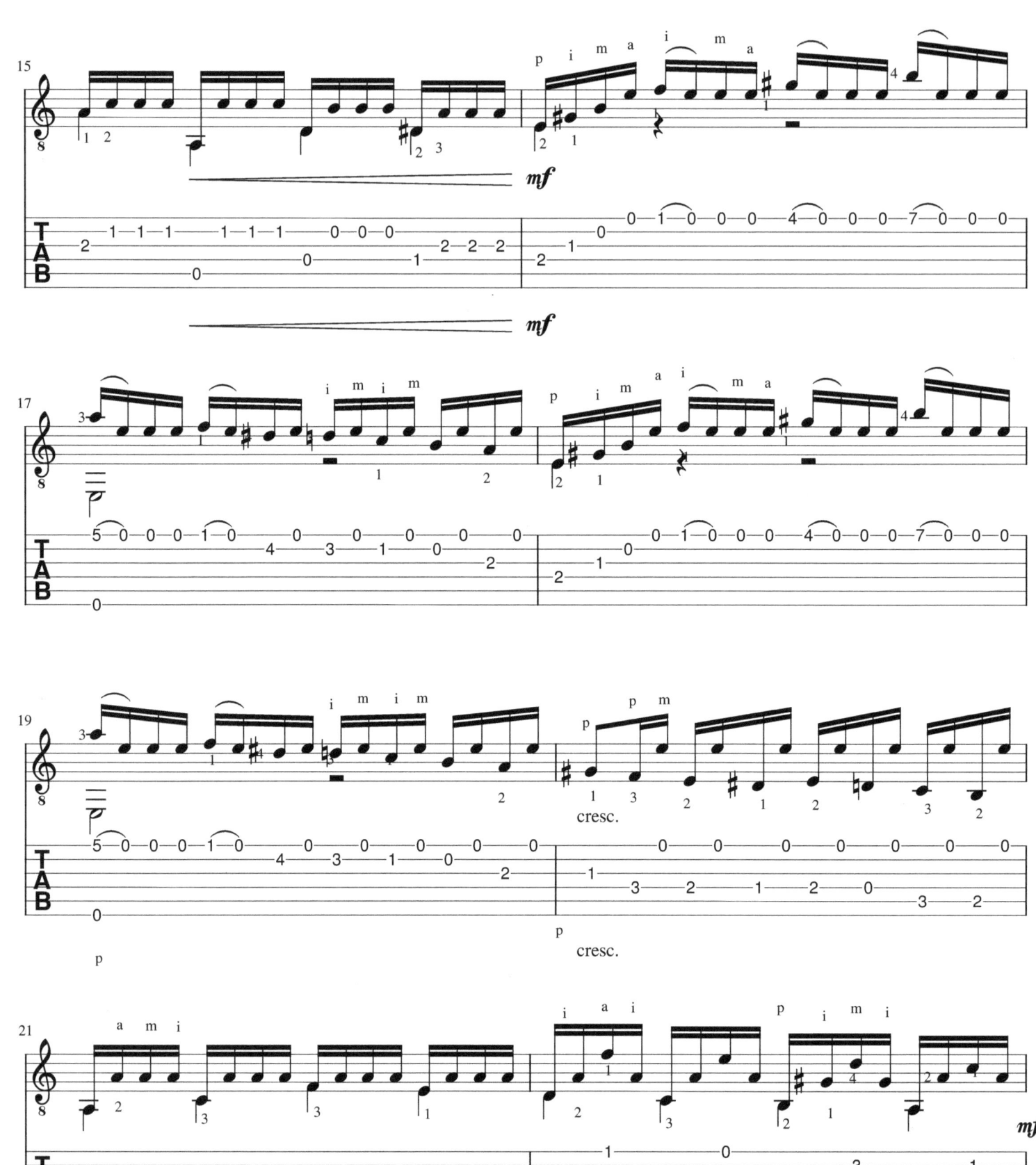

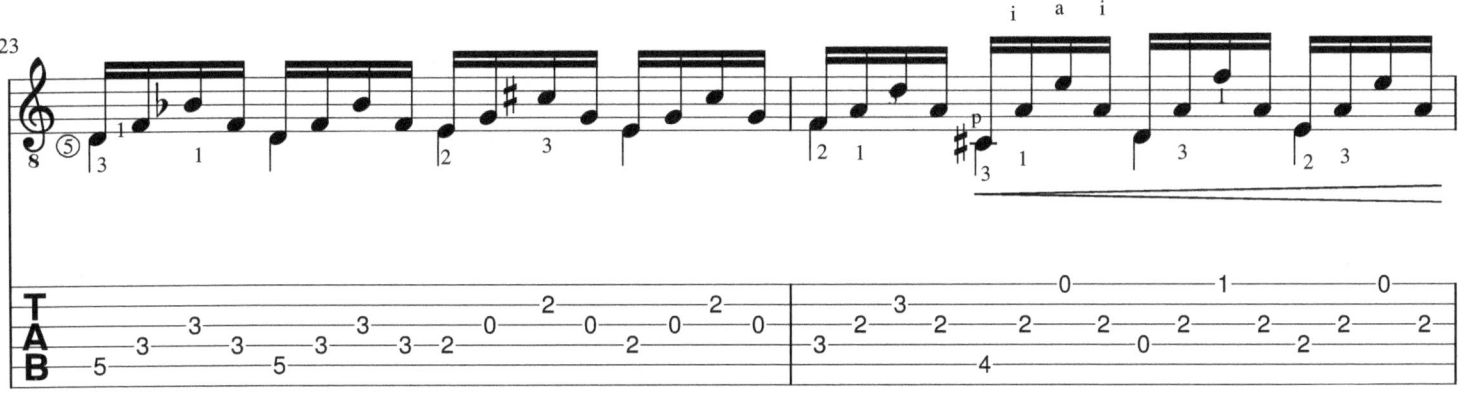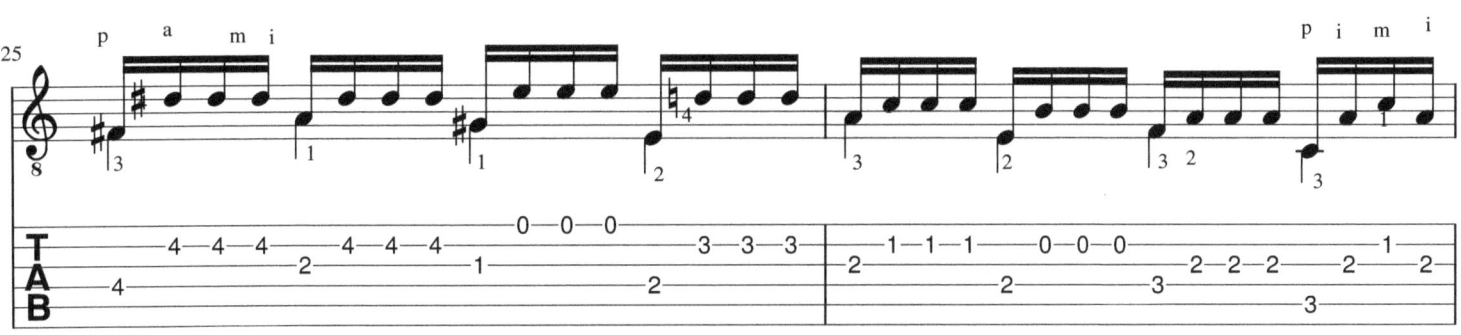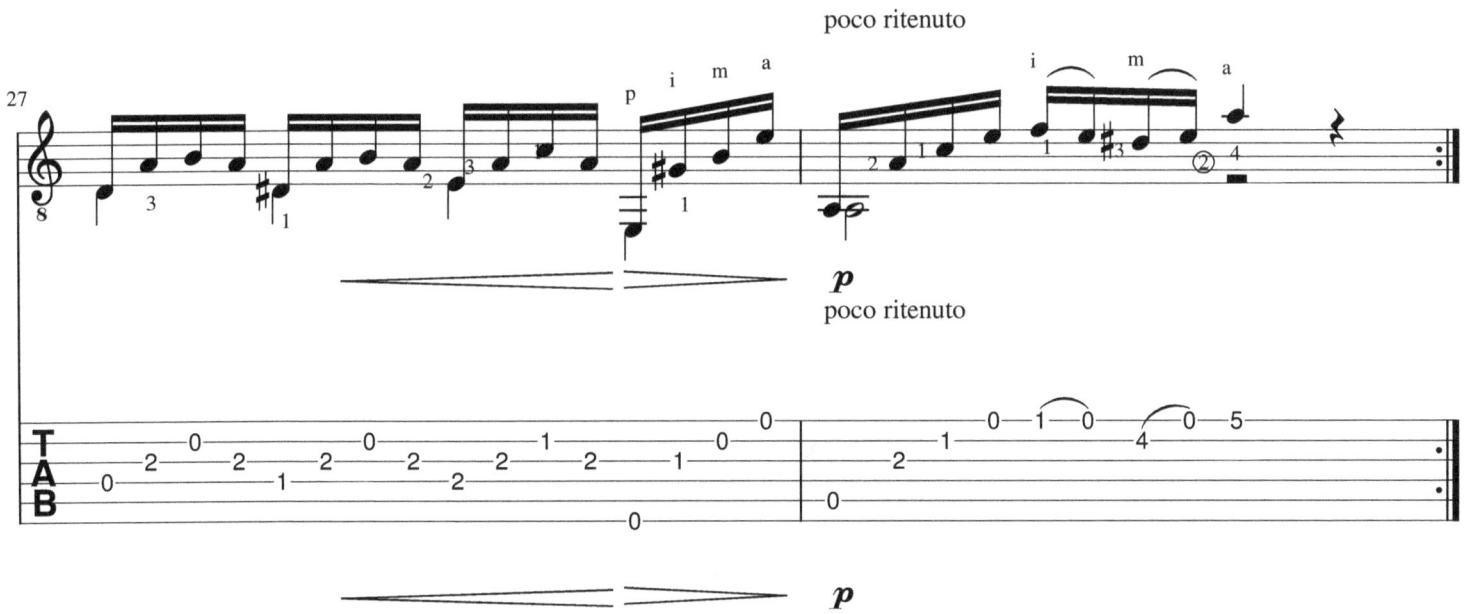

www.ingramcontent.com/pod-product-compliance
Lightning Source LLC
Chambersburg PA
CBHW041808070526
44585CB00026B/2881